W9-CHB-749

PRAISE FOR
MAKING BIG HAPPEN®

By using the MAKE BIG HAPPEN SYSTEM, in less than seven years we've grown our company from a $6 million business that represented a mere fraction of our dreams, to a public corporation now trading on the Nasdaq at over $3 billion in value.

—BRYCE MADDOCK, CEO AND COFOUNDER, TASKUS

CEO Coaching and the MAKE BIG HAPPEN SYSTEM played an instrumental role in shaping the way I lead. They helped guide my decision-making for a decade while we continued to double the business every five years. With their help we grew my company from $40 million to $175 million, ranking in the Inc. 500 fastest-growing companies and the 100 Best Places to Work for ten straight years.

—RICK STERN, CEO, NITEL

Building my business has been a wild ride, and without a doubt I wouldn't be where I am today without CEO Coaching International. Using the MAKE BIG HAPPEN SYSTEM we were able to sell the company for a nine-figure sum at a 32x multiple of EBITDA.

—SARAH DUSEK, CEO AND COFOUNDER, UNDER CANVAS

My business was a TechStars start-up when I first met CEO Coaching International. While working with my coach, we were backed by Launch Capital and NXT Ventures, closed a $6.5 million round of funding, and grew like crazy. By implementing the MAKE BIG HAPPEN SYSTEM methodology, our platform exploded from 1,000 users to 500,000, and revenue grew 13x in less than two years. Ultimately we were able to sell to a multinational retail giant at an extraordinary valuation.

—VICTOR SANTOS, CEO, AIRFOX

The MAKE BIG HAPPEN SYSTEM has helped me grow my company from $25 million to $200 million in revenue in four years. My coach has helped me conquer my weaknesses and it has been amazing! Thanks to Mark and his whole team at CEO Coaching International.

—YI LI, PRESIDENT, RENOGY

I am intimately familiar with the impact generated by CEO Coaching International, and the amazing success experienced by their clients. Having worked with many of the CEOs who have used the MAKE BIG HAPPEN SYSTEM, I strongly recommend it for anyone looking to manage their business to extraordinary growth.

—SEAN MAGENNIS, GLOBAL PRESIDENT, YPO

It was a terrific journey taking my business from $0 to $120 million. By using the MAKE BIG HAPPEN SYSTEM, we reduced our annual attrition from 19 percent to 3 percent, resulting in a $50 million increase in annual sales in two years and a significantly higher exit to a large private equity firm.

—JIM BENNETT, OWNER, WORLDWIDE EXPRESS

CEO Coaching International has helped us grow our business from $1 billion to almost $20 billion in assets under management. After our recent investment from Bain Capital, Carson Group is now valued at $1.1 billion. The relentless focus and accountability of the MAKE BIG HAPPEN SYSTEM made this possible.

—RON CARSON, CEO AND FOUNDER, CARSON GROUP

After a decade of using the MAKE BIG HAPPEN SYSTEM, my team has accomplished results we never dreamed were possible. At one point in the journey of our business I stepped down as CEO, and my replacement decided against using the system. Results plummeted and I was soon brought back in. With the MAKE BIG HAPPEN SYSTEM, we've grown the business from $70 million to nearly $2 billion in sales and have had two successful exits so far. It has given me the confidence that I can run any company in the world. I truly hope you will take the time to learn this system. It will change your business and your life for the better.

—RICH BALOT, CEO, VICTRA

We founded our company thirty-eight years ago, and using the MAKE BIG HAPPEN SYSTEM over the past two years has been a game changer to us. Through the magic of the process and with the help of our coach we were able to sell the business for $340 million.

—ERIC BENSUSSEN, CEO, POWERA

We're pleased to have over a dozen of our portfolio companies using the MAKE BIG HAPPEN SYSTEM, having seen firsthand that firms coached by CEO Coaching International realize extraordinary growth in revenue and EBITDA. Working with them has been hugely impactful for our CEOs in growing their businesses. I would recommend to any CEO to learn the MAKE BIG HAPPEN SYSTEM, and to any private equity firm leader to adopt this methodology with their CEOs.

—TROY TEMPLETON, MANAGING PARTNER,
TRIVEST PARTNERS

MAKING BIG HAPPEN®

BUILT BY THE EXPERTS AT **CEO COACHING INTERNATIONAL**

MAKING
BIG
HAPPEN®

APPLYING THE MAKE BIG HAPPEN® SYSTEM TO GROW BIG

MARK MOSES

DON SCHIAVONE, CRAIG COLEMAN & CHRIS LARKINS

Advantage®

Copyright © 2022 by Mark Moses, Don Schiavone, Craig Coleman, and Chris Larkins.

All rights reserved. No part of this book may be used or reproduced in any manner whatsoever without prior written consent of the author, except as provided by the United States of America copyright law.

Published by Advantage, Charleston, South Carolina.
Member of Advantage Media Group.

ADVANTAGE is a registered trademark, and the Advantage colophon is a trademark of Advantage Media Group, Inc.

Printed in the United States of America.

10 9 8 7 6 5 4 3 2

ISBN: 978-1-64225-327-6
LCCN: 2021914276

Cover and layout design by David Taylor.

This publication is designed to provide accurate and authoritative information in regard to the subject matter covered. It is sold with the understanding that the publisher is not engaged in rendering legal, accounting, or other professional services. If legal advice or other expert assistance is required, the services of a competent professional person should be sought.

Advantage Media Group is proud to be a part of the Tree Neutral® program. Tree Neutral offsets the number of trees consumed in the production and printing of this book by taking proactive steps such as planting trees in direct proportion to the number of trees used to print books. To learn more about Tree Neutral, please visit **www.treeneutral.com**.

Advantage Media Group is a publisher of business, self-improvement, and professional development books and online learning. We help entrepreneurs, business leaders, and professionals share their Stories, Passion, and Knowledge to help others Learn & Grow. Do you have a manuscript or book idea that you would like us to consider for publishing? Please visit **advantagefamily.com**.

This book is dedicated to the countless entrepreneurs, CEOs, and business leaders whom we have had the privilege to learn from in our careers and who have inspired us to make BIG happen in our lives, in our work, and with our families.

CONTENTS

PREFACE

In Mark's first book, *MAKE BIG HAPPEN®: How to Live, Work, and Give BIG*, he shared the four critical questions every business leader should explore on their journey to business and life success. The four questions, called the MAKE BIG HAPPEN QUESTIONS™, are as follows:

1. What do you want? (**Vision**)

2. What do you have to do? (**Action**)

3. What could get in the way? (**Anticipate**)

4. How do you hold yourself accountable? (**Measure**)

Since the publishing of *MAKE BIG HAPPEN* five years ago, these questions have served as a core framework for our coaching practice at CEO Coaching International, where we have helped over eight hundred clients in more than forty countries answer the MAKE BIG HAPPEN QUESTIONS. Our process is field-tested with proven results, with most clients achieving more than three times their industry's average EBITDA growth and numerous clients who, with our help, experienced a nine-figure exit.

Our coaches are world-class former presidents and CEOs who have already made BIG happen in their careers. They did not just read about it or think about it; they actually *did* it. The coaches we have assembled at CEO Coaching International are world class and have built and run major organizations, including Home Depot, Samsung, Procter & Gamble, Goodyear, General Electric, Kendall-Jackson Winery, Tektronix, Telefonica, Xerox, Under Armour, AIG, Brookstone, Manulife, and Sun Computers. We push each other and our clients to do and be better every day. Our coaches combine the MAKE BIG HAPPEN SYSTEM™, described later in this book, with decades of experience as successful executive leaders to become the coach of your business. This is our critical differentiator at CEO Coaching International.

We offer a unique blend of coaching *and* consulting that leverages our coaches' business experience and our proven coaching methodology to ensure your **business** achieves extraordinary growth. What you are reading is a collective effort from the many giants whose shoulders we stand on.

Most of our client companies range from $10 million to $1 billion in revenue and are run by growth-minded founders or CEOs. We also work with several presidents and CEOs who run divisions of multinational firms. In addition, we support many of the leading private equity firms by coaching the leadership teams of their portfolio companies to ensure they get the returns they expect. In all these cases, the business leaders have BIG dreams and are willing to do the work necessary to make BIG happen. Just like a rope is strengthened by many strands, our clients value advice, seek a like-minded community, and want to do well for all their stakeholders. These are the types of companies and leaders that have profited from our counsel.

It is one thing to know how other companies have used the

MAKE BIG HAPPEN philosophy to achieve BIG results. What really matters is how you will use it to achieve stellar results in your business.

All businesses face some combination of obstacles, decision points, and outside pressures that must be managed in an environment filled with uncertainty. These include such things as the following:

- **Technology disruption.** Your worst nightmare could be a twenty-five-year-old who just closed on their $15 million series A round.

- **Shiny object.** The temptation to engage in the "next big thing" takes many CEOs down a rabbit hole that wastes time and critical resources.

- **#you-name-it.** In our socially connected business world, companies face a twofold challenge:

  1. Anything you say or do not say can and will be used against you on social media. Platforms like Twitter have overtaken traditional news cycles and become the source of "truth" for millions of customers worldwide. Companies need to be hyperaware that whatever they post and however they respond, they must be sensitive to the social, political, and natural disasters on customers' minds.

  2. Customers expect more than they ever did in an increasingly digital world. If your customer experience is not adequate, customers will tell you—and the internet at large, too—and they will not have any qualms about airing their feelings. Business leaders cannot ignore their digital brand. If you do not proactively manage your digital reputation online, the internet will do it for you—for better or for worse.

- **Global crises.** Through world wars and terrorist attacks, outcries for humanitarian and social justice, horrific climate catastrophes, and even a worldwide pandemic, businesses face global crises that are completely outside their control. Leaders must develop the resilience to stand by customers and employees as these events are happening; take a stance on these issues; recover internally from these events; anticipate the long-term changes that result; and assume leadership in reshaping best practices in their industries because of these outside factors.

- **People problems.** Managing people is getting harder, demands from staff are rising, and turnover remains destabilizing.

- **Stalled growth.** The dreaded plateau hits every company and most never break through to the next phase of accelerated growth. The median compounded annual EBITDA growth rate of private businesses has hovered around 10 percent[1] for many years.

No doubt you can add to the list based on your own experience. Imagine if you and your leadership team could deploy a process that systematically led you to the answers to your questions, or to the solutions to your challenges. What if this process was universally applicable to every problem faced by any business in any country? How powerful would that be?

That is exactly what we are offering you in *MAKING BIG HAPPEN*®.

In *MAKING BIG HAPPEN*, we introduce the MAKE BIG

---

1   "Fundamental Growth in EBIT by Sector (US)," Damodaran Online, accessed June 28, 2021, http://pages.stern.nyu.edu/~adamodar/New_Home_Page/datafile/fundgrEB. html.

HAPPEN SYSTEM: a step-by-step approach to leverage the MAKE BIG HAPPEN QUESTIONS and drive extraordinary growth for your firm. The MAKE BIG HAPPEN SYSTEM has three simple elements:

Element 1: Establish and Maintain the MAKE BIG HAPPEN RHYTHMS™ to Implement Structure

Element 2: Apply the MAKE BIG HAPPEN QUESTIONS™ to Take Action

Element 3: Leverage the Proven MAKE BIG HAPPEN TOOLS™ to Accelerate Your Success

In this book, we start with a brief overview of the MAKE BIG HAPPEN SYSTEM and then go in depth into each of the three elements. Next, we will provide a suite of proven tools to put the MAKE BIG HAPPEN SYSTEM into practice. If you would like to obtain an electronic version of any of the tools, please visit www.ceocoaching.com/MakingBigHappen. Finally, we will discuss common challenges that organizations might face in putting the MAKE BIG HAPPEN SYSTEM to work.

By applying the MAKE BIG HAPPEN SYSTEM to your specific situation, you will have a field-tested process to drive extraordinary growth in revenue and EBITDA.

Our clients have used the MAKE BIG HAPPEN SYSTEM to achieve an average compound annual EBITDA growth rate of 30.4 percent for clients coached over three years. This means a company that started with us at $5 million in EBITDA ended up, on average, more than doubling EBITDA to $11 million after three years of our coaching.

Would this kind of growth make a meaningful impact in your business and in the lives of all your stakeholders?

Entrepreneurs, CEOs, and business leaders like you are the backbone of the economic engine that drives growth throughout the world. You are on the front line for creating economic opportunity for millions of people. You inspire and lift people up so they can achieve much more than they ever thought possible. You MAKE BIG HAPPEN! There are few things we value more than working with business leaders who are determined to make a difference in people's lives.

Read through this book. But more importantly, "do" the book. We lay out the MAKE BIG HAPPEN SYSTEM in a step-by-step fashion to make it as easy as possible for you to implement it. This system works for hundreds of our clients around the world, and it will work for you too.

Now, go MAKE BIG HAPPEN!

Sincerely,
Mark, Don, Craig, and Chris

FOREWORD

"You are too small."

That was the response I got when I first asked for an intro to Mark Moses.

It was 2013 and I was seated at the corner of a long table at a fancy steak restaurant in Los Angeles. The table was covered with sizzling steaks and big bottles of red wine. Around it was gathered a collection of uber-successful entrepreneurs. I was the least successful of the bunch, but had managed to score an invite from a fellow member of the Entrepreneurs' Organization (EO) forum I was a part of.

Five years earlier my best friend Jaspar Weir and I had started TaskUs. At twenty-two years old we were convinced that a few years of hard work would make us as successful as Mark Zuckerberg. We took $20,000—our combined life savings—and opened an office with five employees in the Philippines. For the first year we provided virtual assistant services—helping busy professionals outsource their lives a task at a time. At the end of that first year we found ourselves living at home with our parents, broke, our business teetering on the edge of insolvency.

We had made friends with other entrepreneurs, all of whom were smarter and more successful than we were. At that time it seemed everyone we knew was raising millions of dollars of venture capital. But no investor would back us. Every time we pitched they would say, "So you are just an outsourced service provider."

Fortunately for us we discovered that our more successful friends were all facing the same challenge—as their companies grew rapidly they struggled to efficiently scale their operations. So we pivoted our business to address this challenge. We persuaded a few of our venture-backed friends to give us a shot. At the start, these companies trusted us to handle their most basic work: data entry and transcription. But, as we earned their trust, we took on more critical parts of their operations such as advanced technical support and user-generated content review.

Five years of grueling work had landed me at the table of that steak restaurant. A few months earlier we had begun paying ourselves $60,000 annual salaries, and I was able to move out of my parents' house into a shared apartment. Our business was on pace to make $6 million in revenue that year. We were a long way from Zuckerberg, but we felt successful.

With that said, I knew we needed help. If Jaspar and I did anything well it was surrounding ourselves with people who were smarter than we were and devouring every morsel of information and advice they offered us. In those first five years in business we relied on the mentorship and guidance of many other entrepreneurs. We were lucky to find brilliant founders ready to offer countless hours of guidance to two hungry twentysomethings. These mentors provided advice and introductions and, in some cases, became TaskUs customers.

With growth came a new set of challenges that our mentors were not as well equipped to help us solve. We had never built a strategic plan. Instead we had reacted to each opportunity and challenge as they presented themselves to us. This was okay to go from nothing to a few million dollars in sales. But as we dreamed of growing into the tens of millions and perhaps even the hundreds of millions of dollars in sales, we needed to develop a longer-range plan. We knew that having the plan was only the first step. We needed a system for developing annual and quarterly goals and a process for measuring our weekly and daily progress toward those objectives. Finally, having built the company on a shoestring budget, we were sorely lacking leadership. We needed a proven method for attracting, retaining and managing world-class leaders.

I had heard about executive coaches from a few friends in my EO forum. There was a mixed bag of results and a hefty price tag to go along with it. It appeared that the differences in results all came down to the quality of the coach. One name that I only heard good things about was Mark Moses. One of the members of my forum said a friend of his had grown his software company from single-digit millions to a multi-hundred-million-dollar exit relying on Mark's management system and coaching. At dinner I found myself seated across from this newly minted multimillionaire. He told stories about how Mark had brought focus and structure to their operations, helped him recruit a world-class COO, and navigated the interpersonal challenges that inevitably arise on a high-performance executive team.

At the end of dinner I worked up the courage to ask, "Can you introduce me to Mark?"

"You are too small," was my forum mate's reply.

I had heard these kinds of replies at every stage of building our business. At first they discouraged me, but eventually I used them as fuel. In this case his response only motivated me to work my network for an introduction to Mark. That introduction came six months later, in the summer of 2014, from another member of my EO forum who had met Mark at a conference and was considering using his services.

I can still remember our first conversation. Mark's deep baritone voice, two octaves lower than his height would let on, asked, "Imagine it's the end of 2020. You are partying on New Year's Eve. You look back on the last five-plus years and you feel awesome. Why?"

My reply was almost instant: "We have built TaskUs into a billion-dollar company that employs tens of thousands of happy, healthy, and engaged teammates around the world."

There was a brief pause. At the time we were still a single-digit-million-dollar company. Had I dreamed too big? I wondered.

"All right, then. Let's get to work," Mark said.

Young TaskUs cofounders Bryce Maddock and Jaspar Weir
meet their new business coach, Mark Moses.

What started as two ninety-minute coaching sessions a month blossomed into a deep partnership. Mark would go on to help us build our annual and quarterly strategic planning process, develop a rigorous framework for hiring world-class senior leaders, and navigate extremely complex and emotional disagreements among our senior team. Mark went from coaching just me, to me and Jaspar, to our entire senior executive team. Members of our team began working with other coaches at CEO Coaching International as well. Mark was there to celebrate our wins, but, far more importantly, he was the person I knew I could turn to in the darkest and most frightening times in the business. With success comes isolation and in some cases Mark was the only person I could turn to.

The role of an executive coach can be so powerful when done well. Here is a person who grows to understand the business as well as the CEO, but remains distant enough to not become entangled in the emotions and egos that can vex an executive team. Unlike an investor or board member, an executive coach has no vested interest, other than seeing you and your team succeed.

Bryce and Jaspar, Inc. 30 Under 30 list members, receiving the Ernst & Young Entrepreneur of the Year award alongside their coach Mark Moses.

In December of 2020, five and a half years after Mark and I began our journey together, we closed the year with nearly $500 million in sales and over $100 million in EBITDA. Six months later Mark would stand with our team on the stage at Nasdaq as we took TaskUs public and grew past a $3 billion valuation. With over thirty thousand employees around the world and the highest Glassdoor score and lowest attrition rate in our industry, we have accomplished the vision Mark helped me articulate when we first met. We are here in a large part thanks to Mark and the MAKE BIG HAPPEN SYSTEM he built into the fabric of our business.

These days I often find myself at a table of entrepreneurs and someone with a fledgling business will ask me, "How did you accomplish all of this?"

My answer is simple: "Find yourself mentors and coaches and don't be afraid to ask for help."

Then I slip them Mark's phone number.

"This is a good place to start."

TaskUs founders Bryce Maddock and Jaspar Weir celebrating their achievement of the ultimate dream for start-up founders—taking their company public on the Nasdaq stock exchange—alongside their executive team and their coaches Tracy Tolbert and Mark Moses.

Hope is not a strategy!

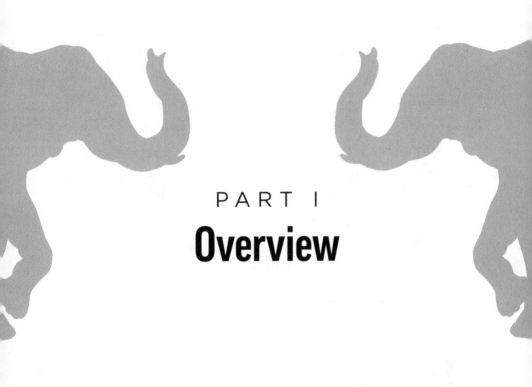

PART I

Overview

A bad system beats a good person every time.
—W. EDWARDS DEMING

Most books that teach you how to build and grow a business are organized around the functional areas of business, such as people, finance, operations, and marketing. Or they talk about how you need to create a vision, have values, develop a strategy, and follow through on tactics. Those things are important and necessary—no question—and we will discuss them. But what is missing from that list is an overarching methodology that systematically reels in every aspect of building and running a successful company and creates a repeatable process to discuss, review, decide, and execute on the activities that will lead to BIG growth in your company.

At CEO Coaching International, we have applied the MAKE BIG HAPPEN QUESTIONS from our first book, *MAKE BIG HAPPEN*, to help over eight hundred companies reach extraordinary revenue and EBITDA growth, which uncovered a proven set of best practices. In *MAKING BIG HAPPEN*, we have translated these hypergrowth best practices into a simple three-step process, supported by over twenty-five proven tools, to show you how to achieve extraordinary business growth.

The key to extraordinary quarter-over-quarter and year-over-year growth is the successful application of the three-part MAKE BIG HAPPEN SYSTEM:

1. Establish and Maintain the MAKE BIG HAPPEN Business RHYTHMS to Implement Structure

2. Apply the MAKE BIG HAPPEN QUESTIONS to Take Action

3. Leverage the Proven MAKE BIG HAPPEN TOOLS to Accelerate Your Success

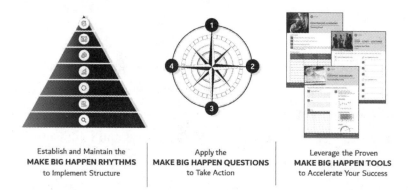

Establish and Maintain the
MAKE BIG HAPPEN RHYTHMS
to Implement Structure

Apply the
MAKE BIG HAPPEN QUESTIONS
to Take Action

Leverage the Proven
MAKE BIG HAPPEN TOOLS
to Accelerate Your Success

A *system* is defined as "a set of principles or procedures according to which something is done; an organized framework or method." The MAKE BIG HAPPEN SYSTEM is a step-by-step set of principles and procedures to drive extraordinary growth in revenue and EBITDA. Just like the iterative process of a machine learning algorithm which leads to the flywheel effect of compounding learning upon learning, the MAKE BIG HAPPEN SYSTEM creates a flywheel effect by stacking daily execution on top of weekly performance improvement, on top of bimonthly accountability, on top of monthly progress review, on top of quarterly alignment, on top of annual planning, and on top of biennial recalibration. The result is a systematic process to build your business and grow BIG.

Deming's quote above serves as a corollary to Peter Drucker's famous line that "culture eats strategy for breakfast." It also pairs well with the age-old adage "The road to hell is paved with good intentions." Achieving great things in life depends on considerably more than a great idea or force of will, vision, or strategy alone, or even exclusively on assembling the smartest and most capable group of people. All of these conditions and more must exist together or be brought together at a moment in time. Moreover, they must be bound by processes that combine their individual strengths and guide them in the correct direction to achieve tremendous outcomes.

Recently, Mark Moses, CEO and founder of CEO Coaching International, spoke to an audience of six hundred CEOs and entrepreneurs. He asked them, "How many of you know what success looks like in your business three years from now?" Very few hands went up. Then he asked, "How about what success looks like one year from now?" Maybe 25 percent of the hands went up. He then paused and said, "If you don't know where you are going, I promise you won't get there."

Jim Bennett, CEO of Worldwide Express, is another example of a client who used the MAKE BIG HAPPEN SYSTEM to produce a nine-figure exit. A franchising company targeting small to medium businesses for LTL (less than full truckload) shipping services, Worldwide Express's revenue was driven by a field sales team across the United States.

When we first started working with them, they had two significant problems. First, their customer service was weak, and that led to high churn. And second, they had no sales leadership and, not surprisingly, were unable to hit their sales goals.

So, we helped the company implement our cadence of the annual, quarterly, monthly, bimonthly, and weekly meetings. With the annual goals in place, we established a quarterly alignment session rhythm and focused on several critical initiatives, including the following: solving churn through a focus on customer service, hiring new sales leadership, and reinventing the sales hiring process by hiring college athletes right out of school.

Following this process over a two-year period, Jim Bennett and the team transformed their business and became the top-growing franchisee in the system. This led to an extraordinarily successful acquisition by the franchisor for a nine-figure price.

Most companies flunk this planning and execution test. Many more fail to utilize tools that drive real value beyond possibly implementing a system that is designed to save them time.

Element 1: Establish and Maintain the MAKE BIG HAPPEN RHYTHMS to Implement Structure

We are what we repeatedly do.
Excellence, then, is not an act, but a habit.
—WILL DURANT

The first element of the MAKE BIG HAPPEN SYSTEM starts with setting up a regular cadence of healthy business rhythms and then maintaining these rhythms no matter what obstacles you face in your business. Our MAKE BIG HAPPEN RHYTHMS help you adopt a set of disciplined, consistent, and collaborative planning and execution rhythms for your business.

We have a saying: "The process doesn't change—only your problems do." Our seven MAKE BIG HAPPEN RHYTHMS are time tested, having helped countless businesses achieve sustained quarter-over-quarter revenue and EBITDA growth, even through a pandemic!

We have discovered that top high-growth firms follow these seven iterative best practices to create alignment and focus among their teams. Collectively, we refer to these practices as the MAKE BIG HAPPEN RHYTHMS.

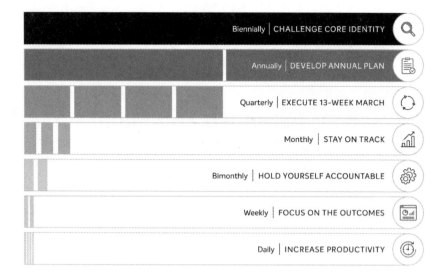

MAKE BIG HAPPEN RHYTHM 1—Challenge Core Identity.
This is a biennial rhythm where the foundational strategic questions like mission, vision, and core values get answered and reexamined.

MAKE BIG HAPPEN RHYTHM 2—Develop an Annual Plan. This is an annual rhythm that sets up the year for success by challenging current strategies and developing new hypotheses that will be tested throughout the upcoming year to drive meaningful growth.

MAKE BIG HAPPEN RHYTHM 3—Execute a Thirteen-Week March. This is a quarterly rhythm that defines a focused set of specific and measurable quarterly company outcomes (i.e., lagging indicators) to drive growth and defines the specific and measurable activities (i.e., leading indicators) that will drive each outcome. We often refer to these outcomes as the *quarterly goals*.

MAKE BIG HAPPEN RHYTHM 4—Stay on Track. This is a monthly rhythm that directs the leadership team to review monthly performance against quarterly goals and make any necessary strategic adjustments to keep their teams on track for the quarter.

MAKE BIG HAPPEN RHYTHM 5—Hold Yourself Account-able. This is a bimonthly rhythm where the CEO and other key exec-utives engage individually with an accountability partner to (a) hold themselves accountable to the completion and effectiveness of their own leading activities, (b) identify the next commitments that spur momentum toward the next milestone, and (c) determine whether a pivot might be necessary, based either on improper initial assumptions or the intervention of unforeseen outside factors.

MAKE BIG HAPPEN RHYTHM 6—Focus on the Outcomes. This is a weekly rhythm that holds the team accountable to tactical execution of the quarterly goals while allowing for week-to-week adjustments to tactics and monitoring of the overall health of the company. This rhythm drives cross-functional teams to myopically execute on the top one to three quarterly goals (i.e., outcomes) despite the myriad of distractions from their day jobs pulling them away from executing on these goals.

MAKE BIG HAPPEN RHYTHM 7—Increase Productivity. This is a daily rhythm that guides every manager to ensure they have the right people in the right seats doing the right things and are addressing potential blind spots.

We will explore each rhythm in-depth in part II, chapter 1. But first, let's look at an overview of element 2 of the MAKE BIG HAPPEN SYSTEM.

***

BUM RAP

We know—the last thing you want to do is attend another meeting. Meetings get a bum rap. But that is because most people do a poor job running them. They call a meeting, chitchat for a few minutes, ramble on with a vague sense of the meeting's objective, and then leave the meeting complaining that all they do is sit in on meetings all day long. We get it—you are busy. Us too. But we are never too busy to establish a rigorous, clear, and regular cadence for quality leadership meetings that ensure efficient communication between us, our leadership team, and our team members.

In 2018, *Harvard Business Review* published a fascinating study of how CEOs of large companies (averaging $13 billion in revenue) spent their time. They discovered that the average CEO attended thirty-seven meetings per week and spent 72 percent of their total work time in meetings.[2] That is a lot of wasted time if you are not doing them right.

The MAKE BIG HAPPEN SYSTEM follows a series of straightforward, progressive steps, starting with the desired objective and working backward toward the specific and measurable leading activities that must be performed and tracked now—and tomorrow and next week and continuously—to build momentum and an ever-faster flywheel effect of growth. Each step in the MAKE BIG HAPPEN SYSTEM requires observation, analysis, responsibility, and an openness to learning and adjusting if necessary. It is at these steps where significant customization takes place—applying provocative thinking to *your* business and *your* unique opportunities and challenges; assessing real-time resources, people, and conditions that affect your ability to achieve the desired outcome; and leveraging the strength of your team and your culture to bring your Huge Outrageous Target into view.

---

2   Michael E. Porter and Nitin Nohria, "How CEOs Manage Time," *Harvard Business Review Online* (July–August 2018), https://hbr.org/2018/07/the-leaders-calendar#how-ceos-manage-time.

Element 2: Apply the MAKE BIG HAPPEN QUESTIONS to Take Action

Judge a man by his questions rather than by his answers.

—VOLTAIRE

In our book *MAKE BIG HAPPEN*, we introduced four critical questions every business leader should explore on their journey to business and life success. The four questions, called the MAKE BIG HAPPEN QUESTIONS, are as follows:

1. What do you want? (**Vision**)

2. What do you have to do? (**Action**)

3. What could get in the way? (**Anticipate**)

4. How do you hold yourself accountable? (**Measure**)

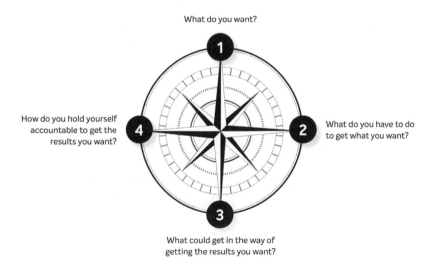

By answering these four questions, you create the foundation for a fast-growing, profitable business. The questions are universal, but the power in this framework is in your ability to apply it to all types of challenges, from strategic to tactical, and all levels of your organization, from the C-suite to the frontline workforce.

Armed with a proven cadence of healthy business rhythms in element 1, you will be well on your way to revenue and EBITDA growth. However, to truly launch your company to extraordinary growth, you must develop the skills and discipline to consistently apply the four MAKE BIG HAPPEN QUESTIONS to every challenge and at every level of the organization.

> **The power in this framework is in your ability to apply it to all types of challenges, from strategic to tactical, and all levels of your organization, from the C-suite to the frontline workforce.**

Part II, chapter 2 provides in-depth real-world examples of how our clients have applied the four MAKE BIG HAPPEN QUESTIONS to solve typical challenges a business will face throughout their own application of the MAKE BIG HAPPEN RHYTHMS, resulting in extraordinary growth. But first, let's explore how to leverage the plethora of MAKE BIG HAPPEN TOOLS at your disposal to expedite your growth journey.

Element 3: Leverage the Proven MAKE BIG HAPPEN TOOLS to Accelerate Your Success

The more time you spend sharpening your axe,
the less time you'll have to spend swinging it.
—AUTHOR UNKNOWN

We cannot overemphasize how important it is to use the right tool for the right job.

There is no need to reinvent the wheel. Through decades of experience, our coaches at CEO Coaching International have assembled over twenty-five proven tools and best practices to jump-start your path to MAKING BIG HAPPEN.

To get the most out of our tools, be sure to leverage them in the context of the MAKE BIG HAPPEN RHYTHMS to achieve extraordinary revenue and EBITDA growth.

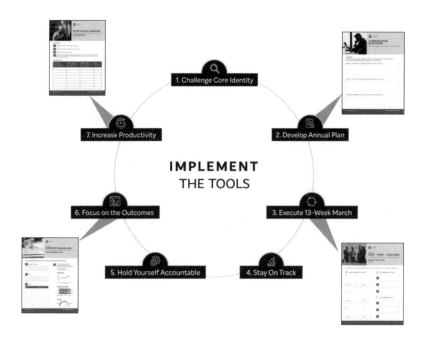

Part II, chapter 3 provides a catalog of every tool, cross-referenced to the relevant MAKE BIG HAPPEN RHYTHM, with detailed descriptions of each tool, how to implement them, and the mistakes to avoid.

***

How to Use This Book

Now, let us lay out what is in the rest of this book.

In part II, chapter 1, we cover the first element of the MAKE BIG HAPPEN SYSTEM: Establish and Maintain the MAKE BIG HAPPEN RHYTHMS to Implement Structure. We will show you what to do before, during, and after every step to ensure decisions get made and results are achieved. We also reference the appropriate tools to leverage within the context of each rhythm. It is all about planning and execution. And while the process is not complicated, it is nuanced.

In part II, chapter 2, we cover the second element of the MAKE BIG HAPPEN SYSTEM: Apply the MAKE BIG HAPPEN QUESTIONS to Take Action. We will provide real-world examples of how our clients have applied the four MAKE BIG HAPPEN QUESTIONS to solve typical challenges businesses face throughout their own application of the MAKE BIG HAPPEN RHYTHMS, resulting in extraordinary growth.

In part II, chapter 3, we cover the final element of the MAKE BIG HAPPEN SYSTEM: Leverage the Proven MAKE BIG HAPPEN TOOLS to Accelerate Your Success. We will walk you through each of the tools we use with our clients that form an integral part of the MAKE BIG HAPPEN SYSTEM. These tools cover a wide range of areas and will help you make smarter decisions and get better results faster. We will describe what each tool is, how to implement it, and tips to get the most out of each tool. In practice, each tool is used on an as-needed basis within the context of the MAKE BIG HAPPEN RHYTHMS described in part II, chapter 1.

Tool Callout: Throughout the book, you will see references to specific tools. Whenever a tool is first referenced, we will **highlight its name** and provide a page reference to the description and use of the tool found in part II, chapter 3.

In part III, we will discuss how to integrate the MAKE BIG HAPPEN SYSTEM into your organization and explore various challenges or obstacles that can get in the way of success. With many decades of combined coaching experience, our partners here at CEO Coaching International have pretty much seen it all. We know what works, and we know what can trip you up.

And here is something else that is important to know. None of what we are sharing with you is theory or our opinion. Everything here is based on our real-world experience, our partners' experience, and the results we have helped our clients achieve. We will share many stories in the following pages that will illustrate how business leaders and CEOs just like you have used the MAKE BIG HAPPEN SYSTEM to MAKE BIG HAPPEN in their businesses.

To get the most value from the book, read it first so you gain an overall understanding of the system and how each part interconnects with the others. Then, leverage the tools as you implement the seven MAKE BIG HAPPEN RHYTHMS in your organization. Finally, have everyone on your leadership team read it so you are all on the same page. Having done so, you will be indoctrinated into a business philosophy that we call MAKE BIG HAPPEN. This philosophy is all about unlocking the growth potential in you, your team, and, most importantly, your business so you can create tremendous economic value for all your stakeholders and personal growth beyond measure for you and your team.

PART II
The MAKE BIG HAPPEN SYSTEM

In part I, we provided an overview of the three elements of the MAKE BIG HAPPEN SYSTEM:

1. Establish and Maintain the MAKE BIG HAPPEN RHYTHMS to Implement Structure

2. Apply the MAKE BIG HAPPEN QUESTIONS to Take Action

3. Leverage the Proven MAKE BIG HAPPEN TOOLS to Accelerate Your Success

Here in part II, we unpack each element in detail to show you how to leverage the MAKE BIG HAPPEN SYSTEM to MAKE BIG HAPPEN!

CHAPTER 1

Establish and Maintain the MAKE BIG HAPPEN RHYTHMS to Implement Structure

MAKE BIG HAPPEN SYSTEM Element 1: The MAKE BIG HAPPEN Business Rhythms

One can ascend to a higher development only by bringing rhythm and repetition into one's life. Rhythm holds sway in all nature.
—RUDOLF STEINER

Growing a business takes great discipline. Discipline to hire the right people. Discipline to create alignment across the team. And discipline to hold the team accountable to achieving the goals of the business. This seems like common sense. Yet too often we see business leaders encourage activity for activity's sake. They fail to move the needle on what is truly important in their business or constantly change the game on the team by searching for the next miracle growth strategy or quick-fix business approach they learned from the last article they read. However, achieving high growth rarely comes via one or two "home run" ideas. Instead, it comes by thousands of "singles and doubles" over the course of months and even years.

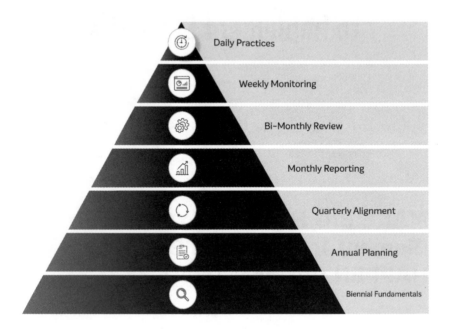

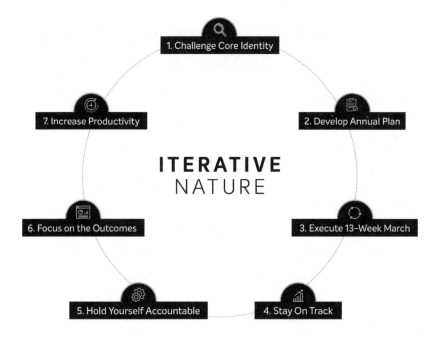

The MAKE BIG HAPPEN RHYTHMS are an iterative set of seven steps that serve as your blueprint to achieving extraordinary business growth. We have seen countless business leaders transform the growth trajectory of their businesses by having the discipline to embrace these business rhythms and the discipline to stick with them, month after month and year after year, even through a pandemic!

Let's dive into each of the seven MAKE BIG HAPPEN RHYTHMS.

MAKE BIG HAPPEN RHYTHM 1—Challenge Core Identity

The value of identity of course is that so often with it comes purpose.
—*RICHARD GRANT*

We start the MAKE BIG HAPPEN RHYTHMS by challenging your core identity. We say "challenge" since most organizations we work with are established businesses with proven market fit and thus have a business model that is scalable. If you are a start-up or early-stage business, then of course you must first establish your core identity. In either case, our best practices and tools described in this chapter will apply.

Core Identity

There are six aspects to the core identity of your business that must be established and then challenged throughout your journey to MAKING BIG HAPPEN. They build off one another in the following order:

1. Vision

2. Mission

3. Company Culture

4. Unique Value Proposition

5. HOTs (Huge Outrageous Targets)

6. Organization of the Future

After establishing the core identity of your business, it is important to reexamine each of these aspects every other year and make any necessary adjustments.

Now, let's take a closer look at each aspect of the core identity of your business.

I Can See Clearly Now: Vision

> *If you don't know where you are going, you*
> *will probably end up somewhere else.*
> —*LAWRENCE J. PETER*

"When the doctor told me I had type 1 diabetes and gave me a script for insulin, I was in shock; I was overwhelmed. I needed help."

At age thirty-six, David Weingard was a triathlete, father, and husband and was in the middle of a successful career at Microsoft. The picture of health. Then life threw him a massive curveball, and he was diagnosed with type 1 diabetes. Scared and frustrated, he turned to the internet to learn more, but everything he found was confusing and not personalized to his specific situation.

Then he met Cecelia, a diabetes educator clinician who worked at the Lighthouse Guild in New York City. Through personalized education, support, and compassion, Cecelia transformed David's life and gave him hope that he could live an empowered life with diabetes.

Cecelia showed David that having diabetes was not a death sentence. He could manage his chronic condition if he had the right knowledge and understanding of the disease and made healthy choices. Because of Cecelia,

David knew he was not alone.

Inspired by Cecelia and energized by the potential to improve patient outcomes, David realized he had a vision to spread hope through low-cost, personalized health solutions for others struggling with diabetes. He quit Microsoft and in 2009 founded what is now known as Cecelia Health, named in honor of the woman who gave him hope. Today, Cecelia Health is helping hundreds of thousands of people with diabetes and related chronic conditions and is on its way to achieving its BIG vision of helping millions of people manage their struggle with diabetes and other chronic health conditions.

Cecelia Health founder David Weingard pushes the limits of what's possible with chronic care management.

The terms *vision* and *mission* have been thrown around so much in recent years that it is hard to tell where one starts and the other leaves off. Here is how we view them:

The **vision** is where you are going long term, five to ten years out in the future. It is an exciting picture of your company, as of a specified future date, that your team can understand and connect to their daily work and key initiatives. The vision is in the future tense and tells your team where you are going in terms of growth and size. It is your responsibility to transfer your dream to inspire others through a clear vision and "catalyze" them to take action toward MAKING BIG HAPPEN.

The **mission**, by contrast, is focused on the present and describes the human value of what your company does. It tells your team and the rest of the world why what you do matters and therefore why accomplishing your vision matters. We will dive deeper into the mission in the next section.

Examples of a Strong Vision Statement

Here are a few examples of strong vision statements based on how we have defined a vision statement above. They set a clear and specific target of where they want to be in the future to inspire BIG thinking.

Tesla: "To create the most compelling car company of the 21st century by driving the world's transition to electric vehicles."

Southwest: "To become the world's most loved, most flown, and most profitable airline."

Victra: "Achieve $1 billion in revenue in 10 years." This was their vision of where they wanted to go when they were an $80 million company. They achieved this vision in just five years.

Grasshopper: "Serve 1 million entrepreneurs within 10 years." This vision inspired them to MAKE BIG HAPPEN. Grasshopper sold to Citrix three years sooner than the ten-year mark.

Why Having a Clear Vision Matters

A clear, bold vision benefits your company in three key ways:

1. **Aligns annual goals.** When you have a clear vision for five or ten years down the road, you can create annual goals that align with achieving the vision. The cumulative completion of each annual goal leads to achieving your vision. Each year's results build upon the next.

2. **Aligns leaders.** Your leaders will pursue their own individual goals unless you create a compelling vision that aligns them toward the attainment of what you value the most. With vision clarity, there is no wasted effort.

3. **Inspires employees.** A strong vision will inspire your employees to keep pushing hard long after the thrill of a paycheck wears off.

So now you know why a vision is crucial for your business, but we still need to understand how to develop one for your company. Fortunately, we have a tool for that! Our **Vision Worksheet** (page 223) will guide you to create a compelling vision statement that empowers you and your team to achieve BIG results.

Going on the Journey: Mission

Without a mission statement, you may get to the top of the ladder and then realize it was leaning against the wrong building.
—DAVE RAMSEY

Kerry Siggins had a problem. Her company, StoneAge, a designer and manufacturer of cutting-edge high-pressure water jetting equipment, was up against existing industry standards that favored decades-old equipment that was significantly less safe for plant maintenance personnel. Even more difficult? The industry was already crowded by preexisting suppliers that dominated the market. Kerry's firm had just designed a new line of automated equipment that performed better and was significantly safer for industrial crews, but StoneAge found itself stymied by old standards that favored the legacy equipment and an industry that was undermotivated to change them.

She could have accepted the status quo, overlooked concerns for worker safety, and opted for the slower growth path that involved a mix of older tools with tepid sales of the new. Instead, she made it her mission to change the industry's standards altogether. Her first step in this mission was to create a grassroots movement: the Global Industrial Cleaning Coalition (GICC).

The purpose of the GICC is to help save lives and reduce injuries in the industrial cleaning industry through the collaborative development and promotion of basic industrial cleaning principles. This mission of creating and evangelizing the GICC will dramatically improve the industrial cleaning industry while also positioning StoneAge as the innovative leader in safety and technology. This is a great example of a mission built to create a win-win environment and inspire people to action.

Kerry Siggins, CEO of StoneAge, and Bill Shires, StoneAge senior manager, standing atop a coker refining unit at Syncrude Oil in Fort MacMurray, Alberta, Canada.

Your mission is an internal and external statement that describes what your company does, for whom it does it, and how and why it does it.

Henry Ford had it figured out when he said, "Wealth, like happiness, is never attained when sought after directly. It comes as a by-product of providing a useful service." Your mission reveals why you are useful. If your mission is simply to make more money, chances are you will never MAKE BIG HAPPEN because you will make money-based decisions instead of value-creating decisions.

> **Your mission reveals why you are useful.**

All great CEOs understand that success is about making an impact in people's lives. At CEO Coaching International, our mission is to build a world-class international team that serves growth-focused companies around the world by delivering meaningful year-over-year growth in revenue and profit. Our impact comes from delivering meaningful growth, which leads to greater opportunities for every employee in our clients' companies.

Mission statements have a long and somewhat checkered history in business, so it is appropriate to question whether they still make sense. In today's world, technology, competition, and customer desires change at an incredibly fast pace. So why should you stubbornly anchor yourself to the original idea behind the foundation of your company? What if a new change ends up making your mission obsolete? Wouldn't it be better for your business to have a fluid mission that adjusts to changing circumstances, emerging customer needs, new technologies, or blue-ocean opportunities? In short, no.

Jeff Bezos, former CEO of Amazon, says that people often focus on what *is* going to change in the next ten years. He said the better idea is to figure out what *won't* change in the next ten years, then build your business around those things. By investing in what won't change over the next decade, you can make longer-term investments that will generate returns for years to come. In a similar way, your mission reflects the aspects of your business that won't change despite the world changing around you. And those aspects that do not change capture the very essence of your business.

Amazon's mission, since it was founded in 1995, is "to offer our customers the lowest possible prices, the best available selection, and the utmost convenience." Amazon started by selling books online, but that was almost like a Trojan horse strategy. Despite losing billions in its early years, Bezos always managed to attract investors because the mission was never just about selling books online but was about helping customers search and find whatever they wanted online with the lowest prices. With this larger mission, Amazon expanded its offerings, which led to year after year of incredible growth.

Characteristics of a Strong Mission Statement

1. **It is timeless.** A mission statement should last for many years. That is why you should put the work in at the beginning, so your mission is enduring regardless of future changes in technology, customers, or competition.

2. **It contributes to your personal life mission.** MAKING BIG HAPPEN is about succeeding in business *and* in life. Your business is your core means to support your life goals. If you succeed in your business but fail in your personal life, that is a poor trade-off. You must be sure that attaining your business mission will contribute to your personal life mission too.

3. **It is consistent with your company values.** You do not need to mention your values in the mission statement, but your values and mission should support and reinforce each other.

4. **It helps your leadership team make difficult decisions.** A strong mission acts as a guardrail that helps you and your team select the best course of action among competing alternatives.

5. **It energizes your employees.** A strong mission motivates your employees and makes them feel that they are not working for you just to pay their bills but to contribute to something bigger.

Examples of a Strong Mission Statement

Here are some examples of strong mission statements. They rally the team around a meaningful purpose and provide the "why" behind their vision:

Tesla: "To accelerate the world's transition to sustainable energy."

LinkedIn: "To connect the world's professionals to make them more productive and successful."

PayPal: "To build the web's most convenient, secure, cost-effective payment solution."

Amazon: "To offer our customers the lowest possible prices, the best available selection, and the utmost convenience."

Grasshopper: "To empower entrepreneurs to succeed."

Why Having a Strong Mission Statement Matters

Here are three ways a mission statement will help your business:

1. **Focusing your own actions**. Great CEOs and entrepreneurs never met an idea they did not like. This "shiny object syndrome" can take your focus off what really matters. Having a clear mission will constantly refocus your efforts toward what really matters.

2. **Guiding your leaders' decisions**. Your mission will help your leadership team make decisions that support your long-term plan. It will foster coordination inside the organization and align all levels of the organization with the firm's ultimate aim.

3. **Improving employees' performance**. A Gallup study on about fifty thousand business units found that strong mission statements lead to better profit margins because they make employees more productive, better engaged, more proactive, and better at serving customers.[3]

Building a strong mission statement and figuring out what will remain stable in your business despite a fast-changing world is tough. Our **Mission Worksheet** (page 225) will guide you through the process of creating a strong mission. Your mission statement is not just words but a commitment that sets your company on a path to greatness.

The How Is Just as Important as the What: Company Culture

Your beliefs become your thoughts.
Your thoughts become your words.
Your words become your actions.
Your actions become your habits.
Your habits become your values.
Your values become your destiny.
—*MAHATMA GANDHI*

Another core identity that often gets neglected is your company's culture. We are not exaggerating when we say culture could be the biggest asset a company can have. It can be a company accelerator or, if not done well, a toxic disaster.

Take Amazon, for example. A key component of their culture is the idea that "every day is Day 1." This means every employee needs to think, act, and work like today is day one of the start-up. That is

---

3   Chris Groscurth, "Why Your Company Must Be Mission-Driven," Gallup, March 6, 2014, https://www.gallup.com/workplace/236537/why-company-mission-driven.aspx.

not easy to do when you have hundreds of thousands of employees and a market cap over $1 trillion. Combine that with the fourteen leadership principles that Amazon continually reinforces with its employees, and you have a well-defined culture that has become a strategic weapon for the company.

On the other end of the spectrum, you have companies that create a culture so exclusively focused on growth and profitability that it leads employees to "look the other way" and engage in fraudulent activities to hit growth targets. Enron comes to mind.

Let's look at some companies that have done "company culture" well.

CEO Coaching International's Don Schiavone was the chief operating officer at Grasshopper until it was sold to Citrix. On explaining the company's culture, Don said, "From the very beginning, we actively nurtured a high-growth culture, but neglected to define our core values. We reached a point, where we no longer liked the culture that evolved, because we focused on growth at the expense of shared values."

So, the Grasshopper leadership team brainstormed what drives growth and how they could create a culture by design, not by default. After some initial fumbling, they decided to simply ask the company's employees what they thought their core values were. Then they went a step further and said, "Give us a story that demonstrates someone in the company living that core value."

Don's team made it fun for employees to participate by creating a wiki where they could submit a story and award prizes to team members who were nominated.

At the end of a three-month period, Grasshopper had collected hundreds of stories with bountiful descriptions of their culture. The executive team sat down and identified the key themes behind the submitted core values and determined which of those correlated to a high-growth company. They identified their top four: going above and beyond, being entrepreneurial, demonstrating radical passion, and working collaboratively with teammates.

With these four core values identified, Don and his team were able to intentionally create a culture of growth that would become a competitive advantage. That effort certainly paid off when the company was able to multiply its profits by ten and was ultimately sold for a whopping $172.5 million in 2015.

As you develop and reinforce the core values of your company, ensure you are not just arbitrarily picking words that sound good or forcing a culture that does not resonate with your people. Grasshopper was successful at fostering a healthy and effective company culture because they selected core values that they knew the team genuinely aligned with.

Left, Grasshopper tombstone announcing sale to Citrix; right, CEO Siamak Taghaddos and COO Don Schiavone celebrating after a successful planning session with their coach Mark Moses.

***

CEO Coaching International client TaskUs deliberately invested in the creation of a culture that wins awards as a best place to work. From the beginning, the company instilled this idea of "front line first." As a customer support company, most of its employees interact directly with the public. So, TaskUs made sure they did a wonderful job of making the team feel valued and recognized.

TaskUs cofounder Jaspar Weir shared, "Let's face it: outsourcing isn't the industry that's got the best reputation. Similar to our clients, we're challenging the status quo. We're trying to revolutionize the outsourcing industry. And we're doing this by obsessing over the employee experience. Today we provide 120 days of paid maternity leave to new mothers at TaskUs. We also provide fully paid tuition for private education for the children of our employees who have been with us for over a year. Another thing we're obsessed with is office design. We've got some of the coolest working spaces in the industry. Chateau Ridiculous is our steampunk main office where airplanes and blimps fly on the ceiling, gears turn on the walls of the conference room, and you can take a nap in a sleep pod. Our other office looks like one of those artisanal coffee houses that you'd see in SOHO or Venice."

How does the company determine if they are actually delivering on this goal of being a "best place to work"? They measure it! The TaskUs team measures employee experience using an Employee Net Promoter Score, which is a survey that they send to their global workforce every quarter, asking one key question: "How likely are you to recommend TaskUs as a place to work for your friends and family?" They manage and measure this metric like they do revenue and profit. This intentional focus on culture has paid off. "People just love working at TaskUs. Our attrition rate is less than half the industry average," commented TaskUs cofounder Bryce Maddock. Glassdoor named TaskUs one of the fifty best places to work in 2019, as rated by its own employees.

CEO Coaching International CEO Mark Moses (far right) standing alongside TaskUs and Blackstone executives at their infamously fun office Chateau Ridiculous.

As one final example, in 2018 when Tesla fell behind its production goal for the Model 3, billionaire founder Elon Musk told CBS he was hands-on in trying to fix the problems. In fact, he said he was sleeping on the factory floor because he did not have time to go home and shower.[4] In 2017, he was fixing problems at the Gigafactory and said, "I have personally been here on zone 2 module line at 2:00 a.m. on a Sunday morning, helping diagnose robot calibration issues. So, I'm doing everything I can."[5]

How many billionaires do you know that sleep on the factory floor? It is all part of the culture that Musk cultivates. Good or bad,

---

4   Elon Musk, "Tesla CEO Elon Musk says social media, artificial intelligence should be regulated," interview by Gayle King, *CBS This Morning*, CBS, April 11, 2018, https://www.cbsnews.com/news/elon-musk-tesla-model-3-problems-interview-today-2018-04-11/.

5   Catherine Clifford, "Elon Musk: Up all night, at times depressed, taking the blame for Tesla production delays," CNBC.com, last updated June 27, 2019, https://www.cnbc.com/2017/11/02/elon-musk-takes-blame-for-tesla-production-delays.html.

he is leading by example, and the rest of the company will follow—or they will leave because they do not like it.

Yet, despite culture being so important, many organizations struggle to create an effective values-based culture. Here is an example. Think about these three company values: knowledge, creativity, and dedication. With some additional context around these words, they could inspire the team and guide an organization to success. Ironically, those were the core values of Lehman Brothers at the time it filed for bankruptcy. This bankruptcy created a domino effect that ultimately led to nine million Americans losing their jobs. Had its executives actually lived and breathed their core values of knowledge, creativity, and dedication, they might have avoided the chain of disastrous decisions that ultimately led to Lehman's demise.

While most companies have a set of core values, they rarely drive company performance. Why? Because the core values are not integrated into the decision-making process of the firm and not lived day in, day out by the team.

Author and consultant Patrick Lencioni said, "If you could get all the people in an organization rowing in the same direction, you could dominate any industry, in any market, against any competition, at any time." Unfortunately, in most organizations, if you asked five employees to share the company values, you would get five different answers. What's worse, a 2017 *Harvard Business Review* article by Ron Carucci said only 27 percent of employees actually believe in their company's values.

> If you want to be a breakout company that makes an impact, then you must go through a thoughtful process to develop, ingrain, and live your values throughout your organization.

So, get this: most employees do not even know their company's values, and of those who do, more than one-fourth do not even believe in them. And we would argue that those who do not believe in your values are probably actively working against you—*inside your own company!* No wonder most companies flatline and never reach BIG success.

Look, if you view values as simply a box you check, then do not be surprised if you end up like Lehman Brothers. But if you want to be a breakout company that makes an impact, then you must go through a thoughtful process to develop, ingrain, and live your values throughout your organization.

If you have not yet established the core values of your company, use our **Core Values Builder** (page 227) to systematically determine what your core values should be.

Why Having Strong Core Values Matters

Here are five ways strong core values can drive your business results:

1. **Develops resilience.** When the proverbial shit hits the fan, it will be your values that allow you to persevere despite all the challenges and difficulties.

2. **Creates a framework for making decisions.** You can always turn to your values to make the tough decisions. Values-driven decision-making creates a decision-making framework that ensures the entire leadership team is working from the same deck of cards.

3. **Engages your employees.** Done well, values can inspire your employees and make them understand that the organization offers not just a salary but also an opportunity for personal growth.

4. **Attracts better employees.** The clearer your values are, the more your organization will be able to attract employees who share them. Clear values also offer solid criteria for you to select employees and leaders.

5. **Creates a foundation for company rules and policies.** Strong and clear values should be the foundation to create your company rules and policies so that they can consistently guide your employees' behaviors. Or better yet, the more ingrained your values are, the fewer rules and policies you will need. Why? Because people will let the company's values guide their decision-making and behavior.

Our **Culture Survey** (page 229) helps you determine how well your company is delivering in eight key areas of a healthy culture, including core values. When you review the results, you can determine if you have the right culture to take you where you want to go or if you need to go back to the drawing board, like Grasshopper did.

The Culture Survey allows you to leverage key strategic strengths:

- **Check your company's pulse.** You may have a sense for your company's culture, but by asking, you will gather the data to tell you what it really is.

- **Set a benchmark.** Your first pass at surveying your team using this tool will set a benchmark. You can do it again down the road and measure your progress in turning your culture into a competitive advantage.

- **Accelerate strengths, eliminate weaknesses.** With good data in hand, like Grasshopper you can determine which cultural attributes support your company goals and which are detrimental, and then develop a roadmap to reinforce the appropriate ones.

Using our Culture Survey tool, you will uncover how well the company is doing in the eight key areas that must come together to form an effective culture.

Stand Out and Be Different: Unique Value Proposition

If you make every game a life and death proposition, you're going to have problems. For one thing, you'll be dead a lot.
—*DEAN SMITH*

The year was 2009 and CEO Coaching International's Jaime Szulc was Levi's global chief marketing officer for the Levi Strauss brand. For seventy-five years, Levi's had used the same simple measurement to size women's jeans—waist circumference. However, through new qualitative and quantitative market research, they realized they may have been using the wrong formula all along.

After reviewing more than sixty thousand body scans and having conversations with women around the world, the Levi's creative team saw that there are many factors that determine how comfortable and stylish a pair of jeans is. Their research and analysis helped them define three distinct body shapes that represent 80 percent of women universally.

Levi's realized that instead of offering jeans based on waist size alone, tailoring them to different body shapes would create a strongly differentiated unique value proposition. Jaime and his team got to work on how to position and market the new product. Ultimately, they launched Levi's Curve ID Fit System, a new line of custom jeans that fit women's bodies better by emphasizing, in their words, "Shape, not Size."

The language used in their branding materials conveyed an underlying message that every female human body was beautiful, and they could provide you jeans no matter how unique your body shape. On one end of the spectrum, the Slight Curve fit was designed to "celebrate straight figures" and on the other side, the Bold Curve fit promised to "honor genuine curves."

Their research also revealed how women wanted to be treated in their retail experience. Levi's seized the opportunity to further differentiate itself from competitors, and as a result, the Curve ID rollout included consultants trained in custom fittings at each store to identify a customer's shape and find the jeans that would be the perfect fit for her body type and style preferences.

By defining a new unique value proposition that was based on shape, not size, and supported by specific and measurable activities consistent with the brand, Levi's built a competitive advantage. The new offerings were a hit globally, and the expanding product line continues to be.

CEO Coaching International's Jaime Szulc, former Levi's CMO, sharing his lessons learned on stage at the CEO Summit.

***

CEO Coaching International's Jerry Swain built and sold a luxury chocolate company called Jer's Chocolates that was the epitome of having a competitive advantage through a strong unique value proposition. Jerry and his team were able to price their chocolates far beyond most of their competition thanks to their UVP. An average peanut butter cup at the grocery store typically sells for one dollar, which translates to about ten dollars per pound. Jer's artisan peanut butter confections earned them happy consumers at thirty-six dollars per pound, and they successfully amassed tens of millions of customers. How did they do it?

"We researched the industry and saw that premium chocolates were growing at five times the pace of pedestrian chocolates. Not just in specialty stores, but for the first time, grocery stores were making room on their shelves for premium options as well," Jerry explained. "It seemed to be the beginning of a trend toward consumer purchasing pivots. Trial and error as part of our learning process, we eventually put all efforts into our UVP. First, we differentiated our actual product. All-natural, best-available ingredients were important. We explained the flavor and quality difference between premium fair-trade chocolate and the specific artisan process we used to make our products. Why a Valencia peanut versus a Runner peanut? What made them the best tasting and best for you? The intrigue captured an audience, and we saw our fan base grow and want more education on our product. Our chocolates did not only taste better, but they looked different as well because they were not molded. When consumers had one of our balls, bars, Jer's Squares™, or Groupies™, they saw all were uniquely a bit different, with slight variations in the size and shape of each individual piece of candy, making them feel like they were handcrafted and homemade."

For Jer's, it was one thing to actually differentiate the product, but more importantly, they knew they had to educate the products' consumers and eventual fans. They explained this on their packaging, website, and all marketing, sales, and branding collateral. Jer's Chocolates became known for their brand story, their packaging, their Jer's Cares initiative of giving back, and the numerous international chocolate awards they won.

The strongest branding component the company had was Jerry's inspiring human interest story behind why he ventured from pursuing a successful high-tech career to becoming a chocolatier. His story includes his long-standing personal interest to "give back" to charities; thus Jer's Cares was born and became part of the evergreen story. QVC, known for being extremely choosey on picking gourmet foods for their programming, chose Jer's Chocolates due to the intentional marketing of their UVP story.

Some version of that story was printed on every product package and was consistent in all branding materials. "What truly resonated with us was a time where we met with a Costco buyer. She brought in her new assistant buyer to the meeting. I was with my VP of sales. The Costco buyer introduced her new assistant and said, 'Jer, please tell my new assistant your story.' My VP and I grinned at each other. Here we were being considered for distribution through Costco, and instead of asking us to talk about the product and flavor, our UVP, the strength of our story and brand, is what allowed us to make the sale."

It is important to note that Jer's did not create a new product. Instead, they just made a better version of an existing product. Peanut butter flavors proved to make up 84 percent of pedestrian chocolate sales (think Reese's, Snickers, and peanut M&Ms). The company just made flavors they already knew consumers loved but with their own UVP.

Many businesses try to be everything to everybody. This simply does not work. Having a UVP backed by research is key if you want to compete, succeed, and stay out of the commodity game.

When Jerry received offers on his business to sell, it was clear to him that the value of the company went beyond the profit and loss statement and financials but was also thanks to the UVP they created that clearly had earned them a strong brand loyalty. In 2014, Jerry's commitment to being different earned him a very lucrative exit to a public strategic buyer.

Jer's Chocolates founder Jerry Swain showcases his award-winning products.

So, how do you define a UVP? A value proposition defines the problem you solve, who benefits from the solution, and how they derive the benefits. Can you identify a value proposition that is unique to your business? If so, that is your UVP.

You will often find that you do not need to hunt too hard for your UVP. Sure, sometimes your UVP will involve something truly creative but not always. It may call upon you to look inwardly at your company—and how you can differentiate yourselves based on the way you deliver to the customer. The UVP does not have to be sexy; it can absolutely be, pardon the word, boring.

But you are not done yet. Identifying your UVP does not guarantee a competitive advantage.

Every CEO believes that their company's products have a competitive advantage. The truth? Very few do. And if you do not have one, it is just a matter of time before competitive pressures will render your product a commodity and at risk for the dustbin.

So, what is a competitive advantage? It means your UVP is *the first choice* for some customers. If you are never somebody's first choice, sooner or later you will be nobody's choice. If your clients choose you only because they are not aware of a better option, you are in big trouble when they eventually find the better option.

Let us be clear: if you do not have a competitive advantage, you better find one soon because your market position is unsustainable, and you are only buying yourself time before your inevitable demise.

An often-overlooked competitive advantage for your business—in an area that matters to many customers—is "superior execution." Many of the products and services that you can invent, innovate, improve, or redesign could eventually be replicated or outdone by your competitors. Just look at Facebook: they basically use Snapchat as their outsourced R&D department and more recently copied the success of Zoom and launched an expanded version of its video chat service. Now, this does not mean you should stop trying to innovate; it only means that you should not lose sight of one simple fact—that one of the things your competitors will find toughest to replicate is superior execution.

For example, Chris Larkins, a partner at CEO Coaching International, shared an example of a company that made an entire line of precast concrete underground enclosures for utilities companies—vaults, manholes, and other containers that housed meters, valves, pipes, fiber-optic cables, and all sorts of other infrastructure. Their business had grown steadily for forty years, but they had suddenly found themselves surrounded by competitors, and their market share was in decline.

After intense discussion, the company decided to ditch its standard line of products and be first to market with a brand-new and highly innovative line (at least for the underground utilities industry), which made it easier for pipes and conduits to enter and exit the vault. They hired engineers, bought new tools and equipment, secured a patent, and hired an expert naming company to brand the new product. The company invited customers to witness "beta tests" of the new vault and launched it with great fanfare. They even gave the product fancy aesthetics, with polished edges that were painted a cool color to appear more modern than competitors' old-school, cold, and gray concrete enclosures.

After much work and some initial success, the result was a complete dud. Not that it was a bad product; it had some features that customers liked, and it boasted several true improvements. However, most of the new product's features failed to meet their customers' real needs—namely, short and predictable delivery times so their construction projects could be completed sooner. In fact, the new product took slightly longer to deliver than competitors' standard vaults. Despite the many improvements, customers saw no need to change products, and they purchased more of the "old-school" enclosures from the company's competitors. Market share slid further.

Chris had firsthand knowledge of this company because he led it through a turnaround after it fumbled the ball in its attempts to recover from the above misstep. The recovery was straightforward and focused on installing people and processes to offer delivery times consistent with the most highly valued needs of their customers. Chris's team revamped the customer service department and gained the reputation for being the industry's most responsive supplier.

They then took it further, investing in innovation that resulted in shorter and more reliable lead times than their competitors. Their plant was soon filled to capacity, and revenue grew by nearly 50 percent in one year.

Chris's competitors were caught flat-footed. Superior execution is difficult, and it sometimes comes with painful choices about people, legacy, identity, and long-held beliefs. For these reasons, competitors responded slowly, while Chris's company racked up millions in sales.

Yes, there are times to "think outside the box" but not to the detriment of delivering the products and services that are most highly valued by your target customers.

In Chris's example, superior, timely execution was more highly valued by his customers, not polished edges and cool colors.

Once you have identified the UVP that can provide you a competitive advantage, you must design the inner workings of your company to support those things that drive your UVP and disincentivize the activities that add no value to your UVP.

Why Identifying Your Unique Value Proposition Matters

Identifying your unique value proposition will help your company in four ways:

1. **Selecting your product portfolio.** If your business sells multiple products, you need to understand which ones have a solid competitive advantage and which ones do not, to focus resources there.

2. **Targeting the right customers.** You may be spending your time and money on the wrong customer segment, whereas greater focus might be merited.

3. **Identifying what drives your advantage.** You can get to the root of your competitive position so you can better leverage the source of that advantage and put further distance between your firm and the competition.

4. **Increasing organizational fit**. Your vision, your values, your goals, your activities, your people: all must be aligned with your strategy *and* your competitive advantage. No single element alone explains why you will be successful. Your

competitors might be able to replicate one thing in your organization but not the whole system of aligned parts.

So, why do your customers choose your products or services over those of the competition? Our **Unique Value Proposition Identifier** tool (page 231) is based on a simple premise articulated by Frances Frei and Anne Morriss in their book *Uncommon Service: How to Win by Putting Customers at the Core of Your Business.* That is, organize your business to *overperform* on those things that your customers value most. The same concept is covered from a different angle by Patrick Barwise and Sean Meehan in *Simply Better: Winning and Keeping Customers by Delivering What Matters Most.* Barwise and Meehan emphasize thinking "inside the box" and flawlessly executing on your customers' basic needs. Of course, both concepts presuppose that you know precisely what your customers value the most, and for that, you need to do careful research.

Our Unique Value Proposition Identifier tool helps you clarify the service or product attributes that are most important to your customers, and through a process of prioritizing and rating, you can identify where your company can outperform the competition on those attributes that are most important to your customers.

Now that you know what is most valuable to your customers, you can develop a bulletproof strategy to capitalize on this value to accelerate your growth by aligning your business model to customer value. As Frei and Morriss point out, you cannot be good at everything. To accelerate your growth, focus on overperforming on the services your customers value the most, even if that means needing to underperform on the services your customers value the least. Often, when we first engage with a client, we see that they have their business models reversed. They have spent years building capabilities in services that their customers once valued but that have now become commoditized and are missing the real opportunities to grow by aligning their business model with the services their customers value now. Better yet, align your business model with the services they will value tomorrow.

Shoot for the Stars: Huge Outrageous Targets (HOTs)

> *The great danger for most of us lies not in setting*
> *our aim too high and falling short; but in setting*
> *our aim too low and achieving our mark.*
> —*MICHELANGELO*

A Huge Outrageous Target (HOT) is a goal so big and so outrageous that it sparks a fire in a team and gives them a way forward to new growth. A HOT is the one goal (or at most two) that matters most. It gives direction to the firm, and failure to achieve it will make every other accomplishment pale by comparison. Having a compelling HOT that drives toward your vision and aligns with your mission is the rocket fuel to propel your team to think BIG and MAKE BIG HAPPEN.

Rob Posner is the visionary CEO of NewDay USA, a home mortgage lender that offers refinance, zero-down loans, and other options for qualified veterans. His coach Sheldon Harris can attest: Posner often has targets; they are huge and outrageous. And together, coach and CEO always find a way to exceed them.

It was no surprise to Sheldon, then, when Posner and his leadership team cooked up their HOT.

Posner's commitment to MAKE BIG HAPPEN RHYTHMS

and TOOLS had already been readily adopted by the leader's executive team. A good habit to be in, too, especially in an industry as "fluid" as the mortgage biz. "Things can change in a heartbeat, and they are outside of our control," NewDay USA senior vice president of finance Eugene Mizin explains.

In 2020, a year filled with wild economic fluctuations, a global pandemic, and a leadership team with its eyes set on a "record-breaking" HOT, Mizin says biweekly accountability sessions were critical. They ensured the leadership team was on track toward their HOT and communicating on everything from marketing all the way down to staffing—*Were there enough people to reach such an ambitious goal?*—and technology—*Did NewDay USA have the technology to accommodate this potential volume?*

Posner and the leadership team kept on pushing toward their HOT with Sheldon as a crucial facilitator and sounding board—assessing all factors along the way, keeping a close eye on all metrics, and making micro adjustments with the same HOT top of mind the entire time.

In October, despite a year more unpredictable than most, Posner and the NewDay USA team arrived at their HOT, then blew by it. In 2020, the company more than doubled its revenue to $300 million, up from $152 million in 2019. Projections indicate the company will serve more than twenty thousand veteran families in 2020 and more than forty thousand in 2021.

Needless to say, Posner and the NewDay USA team have an even bigger HOT for the coming year.

NewDay USA CEO Rob Posner (second from left) stands with recipients of the company's scholarship awarded to children of parents who are serving or have served their country.

How do you determine a HOT for your company?

The key is to look for leverage. Ask yourself, "What HOT, when achieved, would have the greatest impact on our business?" You are looking for a HOT that will deliver an outsized impact on your business and perhaps even help your company grow exponentially. Of course, the HOT must support the vision you created in MAKE BIG HAPPEN RHYTHM 1. Recall that the vision paints the picture of where you will be five to ten years from now. In contrast, a HOT is a specific and measurable goal that ensures you are on your way to achieving your vision. So, be sure to pick a shorter time frame for your HOT compared to your vision.

You must identify the HOT to be achieved in the specified time frame that you have chosen (typically one to five years into the future). Here is where you must strike a balance between setting a HOT that is inspirational and ambitious but not too far out to be unrealistic and demotivating.

To select your HOT, start by identifying the lower boundary, the minimum HOT. The minimum HOT is the minimum result to satisfy you and, if you have them, investors. It should not be zero profit but a profit that would at least cover the cost of capital (let's say, 8 percent return on assets). Then, define the higher boundary, the maximum HOT, which is the result you can attain if everything goes perfectly. This will be overly ambitious and probably unrealistic, as few things go perfectly. After you have found the range, you need to identify the target. The median point is the easiest option, though not always the best one. To help you choose, you could identify a benchmark from successful companies, find out what they have achieved in the time frame you have chosen, and select your target in reference to that benchmark.

In 2019 the leadership team at Arizona-based PCRK Group set a HOT to own and operate seventy-five Massage Envy franchises over a period of five years, through the acquisition of up to sixty-six existing locations and development of nine new franchise locations. Leading the charge was Robert Fish, president and CEO, who brought two decades of leadership experience from Massage Envy corporate as well as Kinko's / FedEx Office. Robert's immediate focus was to put in place a best-in-class leadership team and create an award-winning culture.

Focusing on getting the right people in the right seats

and keeping their eyes glued to their HOT, Robert and his team were able to execute against a roadmap that not only achieved their HOT but did so in a span of eight months. That's right—Robert and his team hit 103 percent of the five-year acquisition development plan across ten states in just eight months. That is called MAKING BIG HAPPEN.

Why Identifying a Huge Outrageous Target (HOT) Matters

Identifying your huge outrageous target will help your company in three ways:

1. **Inspires BIG thinking.** A HOT pushes everyone in the company to think BIG. It creates a shift in mindset from incremental innovation to disruptive innovation that drives leaps in growth.

2. **Identifies the key lever(s).** A well-formed HOT does not just make a grandiose claim. It identifies the specific and measurable leading indicators that will drive the ultimate outcome to ensure you realize your long-term vision.

3. **Provides clarity.** Your team and your investors want to know where they are heading. A specific and measurable HOT provides clarity to everyone and makes the longer-term vision more tangible.

Setting a HOT is often an iterative process. To jump-start the process, see our **HOT Trajectory Tool** (page 233).

When we say "think BIG," how big do we mean? In *MAKE BIG HAPPEN*, we shared that at his past company, Mark made the local news for riding an elephant down the street and straight into the annual meeting at the office to send the message loud and clear that if you think big and act big, you will be big.

One day in 2019, Mark had a similarly larger-than-life idea. He came home from work and out of the blue told his son Mason, "I would like to have a president of the United States speak at our next annual client summit." As most people would, Mason laughed and said that would not be possible. But Mark settled for nothing less than his BIG goal and did everything he could to achieve it.

> **Make your goals huge and outrageous. They will lead to huge and outrageous achievements.**

Long story short, President George W. Bush was the keynote speaker at our CEO summit that year. Like Mark, make your goals huge and outrageous. They will lead to huge and outrageous achievements.

The Right People in the Right Seats: Organization of the Future

What got you here won't get you there.
—MARSHALL GOLDSMITH

Yi Li came to the United States from China with a BIG vision—she wanted to make a lasting impact on the world, and she would stop at nothing to do that.

While she was at Louisiana State University, pursuing a doctorate in physics and receiving accolades for her academic achievements, Yi jumped right into entrepreneurship. Her concept? A solar energy business to help people live off the grid and reduce their carbon footprint.

Though the young student had never run a business before, Yi's unwavering answer to MAKE BIG HAPPEN QUESTION 1 was innate. Yi was going to find a way to make her solar energy dream a reality for people around the world.

At first, Yi focused on e-commerce—designing her own innovative products, sourcing from China, and bringing them to market from her computer. She named the company Renogy and managed to gain traction on Amazon.

Yi had put together the kind of leadership team that any young entrepreneur might find themselves assembling—she filled the roles with anyone she could find. Her VP of operations was the employee who formerly packed boxes in the warehouse. Her VP of HR got the job by being the warehouse employee's sister. Upon realizing that to achieve her future goals, the organization required greater experience and stronger skills, Yi engaged a recruiting firm and hired some top talent.

Revenue jumped from $8 million to $25 million in just three years.

As your company moves through key stages in its growth, you will realize two important truths:

Truth #1: You have outgrown the skills of key people that you have relied on to get you to this point.

Truth #2: You are missing whole new skill sets that you did not need in earlier stages of growth.

For several years Renogy prospered, but with time Yi noticed the growth began to plateau. It was clear to Yi that she was facing the challenge of truth #1: her business had outgrown the skills of key people who got her to where she was, and they were not the people who were going to get her where she wanted to go.

Yi built out the org of the future, and her recruiting team helped her fill the updated seats accordingly.

In a four-year period, Yi grew the business from $25 million to $200 million in revenue. With growth as rapid as Renogy's, the company of the future that Yi envisions has been achieved again and again.

From a dorm room to a global $200 million business, Yi is MAKING BIG HAPPEN by constantly reevaluating and redesigning her org of the future, as every CEO should.

Renogy founder and CEO Yi Li's future-oriented mindset and passion for innovation expands beyond her products into the makeup of her C-suite.

Before you start firing people and jumping into the recruiting process, take some time to create an org chart of what you think the company's leadership team will look like when your HOT is realized. In other words, if you have a two-year HOT, then create an org chart—with role titles—for what your leadership team looks like two years from now. Then, take it a step further and number the order in which you will hire the people on your chart.

Of course, this presupposes that you have already completed the other five elements of your core identity described earlier. No sense creating an org chart of the future when you do not have a vision of where you are heading, a mission to achieve, a company culture that can achieve it, a unique value proposition to enable you to succeed, and a HOT to shoot for.

In the words of *Good to Great* author Jim Collins, "It happens in every entrepreneurial company that there are some people who were perfect when the bus was a little tiny minivan; and when it finally becomes a big Greyhound bus going down the road—the seat is just too big for them. Part of the challenge as a manager is to really be right in answering the following question: Can they grow into that seat or not?"

As you look at your org chart of the future, ask yourself a question: *If we think this org chart will work on our way to our HOT, then why wouldn't it work if we accelerate our timeline and hire these people sooner?*

This is how you challenge yourself and your company to get out of traditional linear thinking and move toward exponential thinking.

There is a huge side benefit to this exercise too. We coach on the idea that you should always be looking for top talent, even if you do not have a position open.

Set a goal for yourself, or your leaders, to proactively interview two people every week for positions that are not currently open. Engage a couple of great contingent-fee recruiters to help feed the funnel and pay them a premium over their regular fees to get "pick of the litter" on any great talent they come across. If you find someone and cannot make room for them, refer them to one of your colleagues at another firm, understanding that there will be a commission to the recruiter. This ensures that your recruiters remain passionate about sending the best people to you.

Why Identifying an Org of the Future and Acting Now Matters

Now, why in the world would you go through all this extra effort when you do not have an open position? There are four big benefits:

1. **Expand your horizons.** You will meet people you never even knew existed and never would have searched for. This may force you to upgrade a role on your team, which could be difficult but best for the business. It will also inspire you to bring in individuals that will take the company to new heights.

2. **Free consulting.** You can pitch the candidates your toughest challenges in their area of expertise, and you will glean great insights that will help you to solve your problems.

3. **Eliminate entitlement.** You will bring out the best in your team through their awareness that their position is not a birthright and that they need to bring their A-game every day.

4. **Capitalize on opportunities.** You can always make room for an A player, especially in revenue-producing roles like sales. By having conversations with potential new talent even when you do not have an opening, you position yourself to identify "rare finds" that add a whole new dimension to the team. Keep an open mind!

Think of yourself as a talent scout and always be on the lookout for the next all-star. Our **Org Chart of the Future** tool (page 235) will help you identify the right seats on the way to your HOT and help you prioritize your actions to make it a reality.

When coach Craig Coleman met cofounders Ryan and Erik Pancheri in 2019, their data-driven live-event ticket brokerage, REPS & Co., was in the midst of hypergrowth. The company had brought in $66 million in sales in 2018, and the brothers were determined to grow even more. Their mission was to disrupt the ticketing brokerage industry by using technology and data analytics to create a more efficient marketplace for live events. Their 2019 financial goal was to double revenue over the previous year.

Craig knew the entrepreneurs could make their big vision happen, but they needed to plan ahead. REPS & Co. had a sizable staff, but the leadership team had significant gaps, and both Ryan and Erik were young—in their midtwenties. Ryan was staffing for the now instead of the future. With a vision as big as Ryan's was, Craig knew they had to make sure they had the right people in the roles to get where he wanted to go, so they began hiring people with the leadership and technological prowess they needed to grow the company they wanted—not the company they had.

They hired higher-and-higher-level people with decades of experience, more than Ryan ever thought he would need, so that these leaders could pave the way and build out their teams. The impact, Ryan said, was instant. For the first time, he and his brother were able to focus on the big picture—scaling, vision, and the future with a trusted team by their side. "The company was set up to run itself," Ryan explains. "We were more equipped to set those high-level goals and have the capable people in the leadership team take care of executing them."

2019 closed out with a big finish—REPS & Co. reached $138 million with a blockbuster year teed up for 2020, supported by a world-class leadership team. Then, the coronavirus pandemic hit. The live-events industry was absolutely crushed. Revenue went down, and Ryan and Erik were forced to lay off hundreds of employees to keep the company afloat. The leadership team hunkered down and got to work controlling what they could and focusing on the outcome they wanted.

"We built and rebuilt new systems and technology so that we can scale again and be bigger than we ever were before," Ryan says. In the next iteration of the business, Ryan says REPS & Co. is poised to operate "in a much more efficient way in terms of people and technology."

Hiring for the future not only brought REPS & Co. the talent it needed for rapid growth, but it also brought in the leadership it needed to navigate through the unthinkable. Though REPS & Co.'s story is still being written, projections are positive, and Ryan's coach is optimistic that his vision can become a reality even bigger than before—in part thanks to their having proactively built the org of the future.

*Ryan and Erik Pancheri with their Org of the Future,
a young but mighty team.*

Summary: MAKE BIG HAPPEN RHYTHM 1—Challenge Core Identity

As we have discussed, the path to extraordinary growth is built upon a solid foundation of six aspects of your business's core identity. Once established, be sure to revisit the core identity at least every two years and make any necessary adjustments by using our time-tested best-practice tools.

RHYTHM FREQUENCY **BIENNIALLY (EVERY OTHER YEAR)**

TOOL	REFERENCE
Vision Worksheet	Page 223
Mission Worksheet	Page 225
Core Values Builder	Page 227
Culture Survey	Page 229
Unique Value Proposition Identifier	Page 231
HOT Trajectory Tool	Page 233
Organization of the Future	Page 235

MAKE BIG HAPPEN RHYTHM 2—Develop an Annual Plan

Plans are of little importance, but planning is essential.
—WINSTON CHURCHILL

About ten years ago, our longtime friend Josh McCarter was running the struggling SaaS business he cofounded, called Booker. His company was generating about $700,000 in annual revenue but burning through $350,000 a month. He did not have enough cash on hand to cover next month's payroll. He had been meeting with various venture funds and was nearing a term sheet that would fund the company with millions of dollars. And just when it seemed like relief was on the way, a terrorist attack disrupted this critical investment. No one thought Josh was going to make it.

Long story short, Josh ultimately grew the upside-down spinout firm into a major SaaS company with billions of annual billings on its platform. So how did he do it?

"We implemented a strategic plan in the business by looking at the market dynamics of our own space along with analogies happening in other verticals. It required us to completely pivot from the space that we originally focused on." Along with the planning, Josh started measuring metrics that were especially important to his business, such as customer acquisition cost, annual revenue per user, and customer lifetime value. A performance-based culture of accountability was taking shape, and he could identify what was working, what was not, then adjust as needed.

The calculated plan Josh implemented in the business gave outside investors the confidence to invest in his company through multiple rounds of funding. The company raised $15 million, $20 million, and $35 million in its series A, B, and C rounds, respectively.

In 2018, the company was sold to Mindbody, the leading vertical SaaS solution for the wellness industry. At the time, Mindbody was public but later was taken private by Vista Equity Partners in a transaction valued at nearly $2 billion. Josh was soon promoted to president and later to CEO, where he led the company's COVID-impacted restructuring, downsizing the team by 35 percent, cutting tens of millions from operating expenses, and ultimately returning the company to the highest profitability levels in its history by Q3 2020.

Mindbody CEO Josh McCarter, on stage at the CEO Coaching International Summit, shares the story of how he grew his upside-down start-up into a multibillion-dollar global business.

Clearly strategic planning is transformative. So, let's dive into the strategic planning process we use with clients that creates compelling goals tied to achieving your HOT.

Anybody can pick a random number and say, "Our goal this year is to grow total revenues by 20 percent," but that is a cop-out. We want to know how you came up with that number. What would it take to double that number? What specific and measurable activities do you need to complete to make it happen? What could get in the way of making it happen? Is it aligned with the HOT of your company where you have determined that 20 percent growth this year is required to achieve the longer-term company vision?

What is your high bar? We want you to visualize it. Imagine it is January 1. A year from now, your company is having the biggest New Year's party it has ever thrown. Your entire team, your friends, your family—everyone has gathered to celebrate this year, your company's *biggest* year ever. You are celebrating because you achieved ... what? We ask this question to CEOs all the time, and they rarely come up with a clear, compelling answer.

Our **Crystal Ball** tool (page 237) forces you to define success a year from now by focusing on two critical yet different aspects of success:

1. **Specific and measurable outcomes.** An outcome is a lagging measure of what you want to achieve. It should clearly define success. All too often, we see examples of outcomes that are vague and impossible to measure or, worse, not unique to your business. Examples of these poor outcomes include "have great customer support" or "achieve high growth." We even see examples of activities stated as outcomes like "implement an ERP system." While we acknowledge installing an ERP system is important, it is *not* the ultimate outcome that your business should be driving to achieve. It is a means to another

end, such as "achieving a 35 percent increase in net profit margin in three years," "increasing revenue by $200 million in two years," etc.

2. **Specific and measurable leading activities that will lead to the outcomes in step 1 above.** The secret sauce to extraordinary growth is to identify the specific and measurable leading activities that are predictive of the outcome (i.e., will move the growth needle) and that can be impacted by your team. The ERP example above may be a good leading activity to achieve operational efficiencies. The key is to make it as specific and measurable as possible so your team has clarity on the objective and line of sight on how it aligns to the ultimate outcome. In this example, we would suggest adding specifics to the ERP initiative like "implementing the ERP system by October 1 such that it provides at least a 28 percent reduction in annual cost of delivery of our services to customers." Classic leading activities are easily found in the sales organization. Assume your outcome from step 1 above is to increase revenue by 40 percent in one year and you have identified an opportunity to increase the number of new customers by adding more sales staff. Examples of good leading activities include "hiring, onboarding, and training twenty new sales associates by the end of Q1," "conducting at least one hundred prospecting calls per week that lead to at least ten product demos per week per sales associate by the end of Q2," etc.

Our Crystal Ball tool will help you articulate the outcomes you want to achieve in the upcoming year and the key activities that will ensure you realize your outcomes.

Now, let's revisit the key question of the Crystal Ball—your company is celebrating because it did ... what? To answer that question, you will have to know your BIG number one goal. Is it 50 percent revenue growth? Is it reducing your customer churn rate from 24 percent to 9 percent? Is it reducing the customer concentration risk of your biggest customer from 35 percent to 22 percent of your gross revenues?

> **The annual planning session is the most important meeting on your calendar outside of your family commitments. Its date should be a bull's-eye on your calendar.**

How do you set these top priorities for the year? More importantly, how do you engage the rest of your leadership team to make sure you are all aligned on the annual goals and are accountable to achieving them?

There is one amazingly simple answer to all these questions: *hold an annual planning session.*

Yet, you would be surprised by the number of firms we engage with that forgo any formal planning process and instead leave themselves in a state of utter chaos, reacting to every challenge just in time and more often too late.

We do not care if it is the middle of July; you do not need to wait until the end of the year to do your annual planning session. Start now, as every day of delay is a day of decay.

The annual planning session is the most important meeting on your calendar outside of your family commitments. Its date should be a bull's-eye on your calendar.

At this session, you will reflect on the past year and determine the key goals and initiatives for the year ahead. You will get your entire leadership team aligned on the three to five BIG goals and company-wide initiatives that must get accomplished over the next twelve months. And you will get clear on exactly how those BIG goals and initiatives will get accomplished, who is responsible, and what metrics you will monitor to ensure you are on track.

There is significant nuance required to define the above properly, and the correct answers often come only after heavily facilitated discussion. It is entirely possible that you may decide that your company has been pursuing the wrong goal all along or selling itself short or setting itself up for unnecessary disappointment. Similarly, you may find that the company requires a stronger foundation to pursue its HOT—built upon a new or clearer vision, an upgraded team or structure, or a reconfigured unique value proposition by revisiting the company's core identity discussed in the first MAKE BIG HAPPEN RHYTHM.

The MAKE BIG HAPPEN SYSTEM is premised upon the principle that to do something you have never accomplished—namely, to achieve an outcome that by definition will be "new" to you—you must look at things in ways that are also new to you. The second MAKE BIG HAPPEN RHYTHM launches with the annual planning session, where a clearly defined, specific, and measurable long-term goal (your HOT) is broken into more immediate milestones for the upcoming year.

The absence of common definitions of success can otherwise turn strategic planning meetings into the "all talk, no impact" sessions that most of our clients experienced prior to working with us. Without it, how will you know if you are winning? If you do not keep track at all, it is anybody's guess. By contrast, if you are only measuring outcomes (e.g., number of new clients added) instead of leading activities (e.g., the actual completion—at targeted frequencies—of those actions that result in adding more clients), then you have no way to hold yourselves accountable in real time. All you can do is look through the rearview mirror.

No matter the size or stage of your company, get an annual planning session on the calendar. Block out at least three days, including a day of travel on either side. This is the biggie, and it is nonnegotiable.

Annual Planning Session

Here is how to prepare for, execute, and follow through on the meeting that sets the agenda for your company's whole year. Let's start with the three essential tasks the CEO needs to execute ahead of time so that the annual planning session is as comprehensive and as effective as possible.

Prior to the Meeting

The more prepared you and your leadership team can be going into the meeting, the more productive and effective the meeting will be coming out of it. It is that simple. Here are the three pre-meeting tasks:

1. **Think about your goals for the year ahead.**

   We are going to get to the nitty-gritty details of how your company's doing, what it can do better, and how to run the meeting, but right now, forget about all that. Instead, break out your crystal ball and ask yourself: "What do I want?" It is the first of the four MAKE BIG HAPPEN QUESTIONS. As you gaze into your crystal ball, what future are you envisioning? What is your BIG goal? Where do you want to be at the end of next year? How will that goal feed into a three-year goal? Or five-year HOT?

   If you cannot picture yourself a year from now celebrating with your whole company because you achieved _____, then your _____ is not BIG enough or specific enough.

This pre-meeting envisioning is a crucial step in the annual planning process. So, give yourself the time and space you need to see your company's future as clearly as possible. There is no point in holding a planning session if you do not have a BIG goal worth planning for.

2. **Assign the pre-meeting homework.**

Get your leadership team together and prep them for the upcoming planning session. Share your ten-thousand-foot view of the year ahead and share some context on where you see your company and your industry heading. This is not about "telling" your team what to think; rather, it is about sharing your perspective based on information that only you—as the CEO—have.

At the end of this pre-meeting, distribute the following questions and ask your leaders to send their answers to your assistant, who will then collate them into the **Annual/ Quarterly Planning Session Pre-Work** (page 239):

- What went right over the past twelve months?

- What went wrong over the past twelve months?

- What did we learn over the past twelve months?

- How did we do on our annual goals compared to how we said we would do?

- How did we do on the specific and measurable activities we were keeping score on that we said would lead us to the outcome that we wanted?

- What are our greatest opportunities next year?

- What are our greatest challenges?

- What is the number one goal you think we could achieve next year that would have the biggest impact on our company's growth?

Their answers—and yours—are going to form the blueprint for what you cover at your annual planning session.

3. **Hire a facilitator.**

The annual planning session is not you on stage wearing a black turtleneck and pontificating about the company's future. It is work—work that you need to be participating in, not orchestrating.

Hiring a third party to facilitate your annual planning session is always a best practice. When you sit elbow to elbow with the rest of your leadership team, discussing the same issues, confronting the same problems, and working together toward solutions, you're sending a powerful message: "We're all in this together. I am responsible for what is working and what is not working the same as you are. We can all do better, including me."

Even though you may be tempted to facilitate the planning meeting yourself—do not. If the CEO facilitates it, the other leaders might consciously or subconsciously feel compelled to agree with you, and it might limit the free flowing of thoughts to some degree. Also, you will be torn between being CEO and a participant of the meeting versus being the facilitator. And you will not do either of those roles well.

An expert third-party facilitator will know how to probe when your team is not fully bought in, dig for root causes of issues being discussed, insist on defining measurable activities and outcomes for key initiatives, and call out the elephant in the room that everyone is avoiding. This expertise makes all the difference between a superficial, inconsequential meeting and a true planning session that powerfully aligns and energizes your team around the goals for the coming year and the key activities required to get there.

Even better, take this meeting off site to a location that is inspiring, is conducive to strategic thinking, and feels like a reward for the accomplishments achieved the year before. For some of our clients, we traveled to resort locations. You do not have to go that far, but at least get out of the office, perhaps to a local conference center. You want to minimize your normal day-to-day distractions so you can focus on the big task at hand.

Many of our clients have testified that an outside facilitator is a must-have. In the words of one particular CEO, "Our coach facilitated a handful of quarterly planning sessions for us last year, which we loved. They were amazing. After getting familiar with the process, I decided I was ready to run it myself, so I let my coach know I wouldn't be needing him anymore, and I ran that meeting. Oh, how I wish I hadn't done that. It was night and day from the previous sessions, so much less valuable from not being able to participate myself. The members of my team couldn't contribute to the conversation with the same level of candor. We developed to-dos instead of initiatives. We fell behind and had a lot of damage to undo in the form of misalignment. You can bet I called my coach back up, letting him know he'd be running all future sessions. We bring him in four times a year."

During the Meeting

Now that you, your leadership team, and your professional outside facilitator have completed all the necessary pre-work, it is time to talk about how an effective one- or two-day annual planning session works. Let's look in detail at the six parts of this meeting.

Introduction

Start with a short icebreaker exercise to warm up the room. Once you have had a good laugh or meaningful reflective moment together, it is time to align expectations for the day. You have all done the pre-work and have come into the meeting with your own ideas and expectations. Now, a skilled facilitator will ask each attendee to share their expectations, and then he will distill them to a set that everyone is aligned with. By the end of this brief discussion, it should be clear to everybody "what success looks like" for this meeting.

It is also particularly important to set ground rules for the meeting. Here are several that typically show up in the sessions we facilitate:

1. **Agreement is optional; commitment is not.** You will have strong opinions in the room, and not everyone will agree with the direction that is ultimately decided upon. But once that decision is made or that direction is set, everyone needs to commit to it. And if for some reason one of your leaders cannot in good conscience commit to it, then they need to resign.

2. **Be in the room.** Yes, this is basic but bears reminding. Focus on the task at hand, not on checking your emails.

3. **Wear two hats.** As a functional leader, you are working "in" the business and giving your feedback as it relates to your functional role. But then put an "outside advisor" hat on too. Step outside your functional role as if you were an independent board member. With that perspective, what advice and guidance would you provide over the course of the meeting?

4. **Do not leave it unsaid.** Look, everything is on the table here. Be transparent, tell it the way you see it, but do it in a professional and respectful way. And if you happen to be on the receiving end of some feedback or pushback, do not get defensive. Receive it in the spirit in which it is delivered— everyone is trying to get to the best outcome.

5. **Follow the three Cs of communication.** Be clear, concise, and compelling. We are looking for dialogue, not monologues.

6. **No "rabbit chasing."** Keep separate track of issues or topics that are important but not appropriate to discuss at this meeting. Add them to the "parking lot."

Twelve-Month Review

The first working section of the annual planning session is a review of the past twelve months. The goal of this section is to hold everyone accountable, to celebrate victories and challenges overcome, and to remind the team about the challenges that still need to be faced. Remember the pre-meeting homework we asked you to do? This is the point in the meeting where you review every one of those pre-meeting questions.

As you review the pre-work work, what pops out? What patterns are apparent? What is becoming clear?

Even though it is in the rearview mirror, take a moment to review how you did compared to how you said you would do. On a scale of one to ten, how well did you execute on last year's plan? What could you do to improve your execution this year? Are there any problems or issues from the past year that will need to be resolved this year? Dust off the **Secret Ballot** tool (page 241) to uncover areas of misalignment across the leadership team. The following are often also asked by secret ballot:

1. On a scale of one to ten, how well does the company live its core values?

2. On a scale of one to ten, what is your perception of the culture of the company?

3. On a scale of one to ten, how well do we internally communicate as a company?

4. On a scale of one to ten, how satisfied are you in your current position?

5. On a scale of one to ten, how strong is the company's management team (or another team)?

6. What is the company's "weakest link" (or Achilles' heel)?

7. What is the number one problem we need to address right now?

8. Is there something that we are "ignoring the obvious" about?

One of the underappreciated benefits of the twelve-month review is it helps you compound your learning. By answering the "What did we learn?" question and memorializing those learnings, you can leverage those insights into greater success in the years ahead. Too many companies never take a moment to nail down what they learned and, as a result, are doomed to repeat mistakes or let up on what has been working.

Strategic Planning

The goal of the second working section of the annual planning session is to formulate or revise the strategic positioning of the company and to strategically evaluate what each leader can do to get better. There are three important exercises here.

First, review your unique value proposition from MAKE BIG HAPPEN RHYTHM 1. Is it really that unique? Is it defensible going forward? Are competitors catching up and minimizing your advantage? Without a unique value proposition, it will be hard to generate sustainable double-digit growth.

Second, answer the **Provocative Questions** (page 243). These questions can help you identify initiatives that lead to achieving your desired yearly goal. It follows a bottom-up approach.

One of our clients, Kevin Duffy, is the CEO of Sound United. When we met him in 2015, the company's revenue had plateaued at $152 million with EBITDA of about $13 million. The company had been underperforming for the past two years.

We held a two-day strategic planning session with the Sound United leadership team, where they completed the "Three Provocative Questions" exercise that ultimately transformed the business.

The exercise presents a scenario that requires you to refresh your thinking and pretend you are starting your business from scratch. Kevin and his team were asked, "Imagine you are starting a new company that would compete with the one you operate now."

With that concept in mind, the team answered these questions:

1. What am I doing now that I would stop doing in my new company?
2. What am I not doing now that I would start doing in my new company?
3. How would I compete to try to put my old company out of business?

The Sound United leadership team wrote down the name of a fictitious company on a whiteboard and brainstormed to identify initiatives that could address the issues they surfaced in answering the questions. From there, their facilitator helped them assess the potential of each initiative in terms of its impact and effort and then assigned a clear owner to each initiative.

The exercise resulted in a full reimagination and reinvention of the business. After staring at what they designed on the whiteboard at the front of the room, the consensus was, "That's pretty cool. We want that company instead of the one we have."

Over the next few years, Sound United systematically pursued creating the desired company of the future through a disciplined adherence to the MAKE BIG HAPPEN SYSTEM. Ultimately, the company did a complete reorganization from one global centralized department-based P&L to a decentralized "business within a business" brand-led P&L.

In 2020, Sound United revenues were $798 million with EBITDA of $113 million. That is the power of this three-question exercise—revenue growth of 419 percent and over eight times EBITDA growth in five years.

CEO Kevin Duffy speaking on Sound United's vision and strategy.

Third, work on improving the performance of each person on the leadership team. Yes, we have this under strategic planning because each person on your leadership team is a strategic asset of the company. The better they can perform, the better your company will perform. Refer to MAKE BIG HAPPEN RHYTHM 7 for skills development tools.

Here is where some senior leadership humility comes into play. Go around the room and ask each person to answer three questions. First, what they should stop doing; second, what they should start doing now to improve their effectiveness; and third, the highest-payoff activity (HPA) that they should continue to do. Note that your HPA is defined as the *one* thing that, if you did more of it each day, would have the greatest impact on your success. Also, keep in mind that the "stop-doing" list does not mean the organization stops doing it. Rather, it means *you* stop doing it. This often involves delegating lesser-payoff activities to others. Our **Stop-Start-Continue** tool (page 245) helps leaders prepare their answers to these questions. This is a simple but powerful exercise to help ensure bad practices get ditched and important new activities get added. It is easy to get into a rut, and this exercise will force your team to drop old habits and add new and better ones.

These three exercises will prime your thinking and set you up for success as you move to the next part of the meeting—turning strategy into actionable activities.

From Strategy to Execution

Now it is time to revisit your HOT from MAKE BIG HAPPEN RHYTHM 1 and complete the HOT Trajectory tool we describe in that section if you have not already done so. Our HOT Trajectory tool will help you establish the one to two goals that must be accomplished for the year to position you to achieve your HOT in future years. A seasoned facilitator will challenge the entire leadership team to pressure test the annual goals and then change the mindsets of the team to think BIG. To this end, we often walk our clients through several exercises:

- Revenue Bridge

- Sensitivity Analysis

- Sales Roadmap, Plan, and Playbook

- Cash Bridge

Let's walk through each of these exercises and show how they help you and your management team to pressure test your goals and develop specific and measurable execution plans.

Revenue Bridge

A revenue bridge is a type of waterfall bar chart that starts with a firm's current annual revenue (referred to as the baseline) and adds to or subtracts from this baseline revenue in subsequent bars based on forecasts for various unit economic drivers that add revenue to or subtract revenue from baseline and results in a projection of the revenue for the upcoming year. The bars of the chart tend to look like a waterfall in that they "cascade" up or down like a waterfall.

Here is a classic example of a price/volume revenue bridge for one product line:

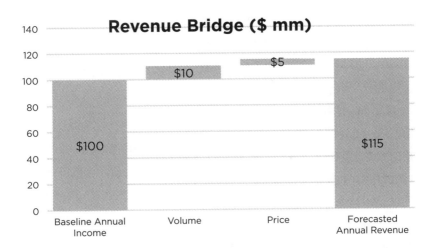

Notice that the forecasted change in total revenue of $15 million is made up of two separate unit economic impacts: (1) $10 million due to volume and (2) $5 million due to price. Also, see how the bars cascade up to the forecasted revenue. They appear like a waterfall from the forecasted revenue back to baseline revenue.

The revenue bridge provides a visual representation of your growth strategy to confirm the feasibility of your goals and help determine how to prioritize your resources. It forces you and your finance team to uncover and understand the unit economics of your business from two important perspectives:

1. Historic growth drivers: detailed analysis of the historic economics of your business, especially around customer purchasing behaviors, to understand trends in customer retention/churn and average lifetime value by customer segment, to paint a picture of whether revenue is naturally expanding or contracting.

2. Projected growth drivers: detailed model of forecasted growth drivers based on opportunities or challenges that will impact your future unit economics, such as organic and inorganic growth opportunities, upsell and cross-sell opportunities, etc.

> A skilled CFO should be able to model the unit economics of their business and present a revenue bridge to enable them to see where the focus should be over the coming year to achieve their revenue goals.

For example, how does unit price change in relation to volume? What is your "per store" foot traffic, and how is it changing? What is your conversion rate per marketing campaign, and when will each channel saturate? The types of questions you ask depend on your industry. A skilled CFO should be able to model the unit economics of their business and present a revenue bridge to enable them to see where the focus should be over the coming year to achieve their revenue goals. Here are some of the various levers that you can pull in your business to grow revenues:

- Price or volume increases with existing customers

- Acquisition of new customers, based on your marketing plan

- The launch of new products and services

- Improvement in KPIs

Do not forget to add in the factors that lead to negative growth, such as customer attrition, price compression, loss of market share, etc.

Our highest-growing clients take the revenue bridge analysis to a whole new level through a sensitivity analysis.

Sensitivity Analysis

A sensitivity analysis allows you to estimate how variable inputs affect potential target outcomes. It is also referred to as a "what-if" analysis and often requires business model simulations to determine how the input variables affect the business outcomes of revenue and profit.

Let's take a simple example of a business-to-business service sold via the internet. The CMO wants to understand the impact of site traffic on total sales. Through historic growth driver analysis, she determines that a 10 percent increase in site traffic results in a 2 percent increase in purchase volume for their core product offering. Their current average revenue per unit is $10,000, and their current baseline annual volume is fifty thousand units. Using this historic data, she builds a forecast model that predicts what happens when we increase site traffic and presents the model in the form of a sensitivity analysis as follows:

One-Dimensional Sensitivity Analysis

Average Revenue Per Unit (ARPU): $10,000
Baseline Annual Volume: $50,000

	CHANGE IN SITE TRAFFIC					
	1%	5%	10%	15%	20%	25%
REVENUE ($ MM)	501.0	505.0	510.0	515.0	520.0	525.0
	30%	35%	40%	45%	50%	
REVENUE ($ MM)	530.0	535.0	540.0	545.0	550.0	

Thanks to traffic experiments she ran during the past quarter, she is confident that she can increase site traffic by 20 percent for the year, which would add $25 million in revenue for the year. During the planning session, their business coach challenges the leadership team to think BIG, and they identify two promising new channels that could add another 10 percent to site traffic. They leave the planning session with a new annual goal of a 30 percent increase to site traffic that is expected to add $30 million in revenue. Yes, we realize that this is an oversimplification. Sophisticated readers will note that unless the firm has zero churn, we will fall short of our revenue goal despite hitting our traffic goal. This is where iterative analysis comes into play. Do not let the difficulty of the challenge stop you from taking the first step. The above analysis is the first step. Next, we would challenge the team to uncover their unit churn/retention data and update the model. As the team gets comfortable with the model, we would suggest adding a second dimension. In the above example, we would challenge the team to run pricing tests and see how the change in unit price affects unit sales volume. Finally, we would have the client create a two-dimensional model showing how revenue is impacted by changes in site traffic and unit price.

The key to a meaningful sensitivity analysis is to identify the most significant assumptions that affect your revenue and profit. The most important value of a sensitivity analysis comes from the healthy discussion about the data that a competent facilitator should drive. All too often we see leadership teams enter a planning session with an incremental growth mindset and cannot seem to get out of their own way and take advantage of the abundance of opportunities that surround them. In these cases, we use the sensitivity analysis to show them how seemingly small changes to key unit economic drivers can have massive impacts on revenue and EBITDA.

In a recent planning session, our client Rich Balot and his team at Victra Wireless executed a sensitivity analysis that revealed that a $1 increase in the gross profit of mobile phone accessories, a second-tier product offering, would yield a $7 million increase to EBITDA for that year. That is *just a $1 change* per customer—imagine what a $10 change input would do! A properly conducted sensitivity analysis in the arms of a competent business coach goes a long way to pushing the team to change their mindsets on the opportunities that lie before them.

Sales Roadmap, Plan, and Playbook

Thanks to the insights provided by your revenue bridge and sensitivity analysis, you will likely identify huge opportunities for massive growth through organic sales. To help your leadership team assess these opportunities and then execute on them, we have developed our **Sales Roadmap, Plan, and Playbook** tool (page 249).

The Sales Roadmap, Plan, and Playbook (SRPP) tool encompasses your actionable sales strategy by defining the following:

- **Roadmap:** defines and documents all of the assumptions pertaining to the sources of your organic growth and identifies the clearest path to achieve your sales goals

- **Plan:** outlines all the specifics behind the roadmap's assumptions and clearest path, creating an executable blueprint to achieve the roadmap

- **Playbook:** details the critical leading activities to execute the plan, including the funnel and scorecard of each activity, and a script that offers guidance on how each activity should be performed

Each component of the revenue bridge should have its own SRPP. Taken together, all the SRPPs form the foundation of an executable, winning sales strategy.

COMPONENT	DEFINITION	EXAMPLES
ROADMAP	All the assumptions about the "Clearest Path" to achieve your Sales Goal	"$1M in new business will come from 20 new customers at an average of $50K each: 2 in Q1, and 6 each in Q2/Q3/Q4."
PLAN	The specifics behind those assumptions: THESE Markets, THESE Customers, THESE Products, THESE PRICES, etc.	"We will focus on dealers over X size servicing THESE customers with THESE products in the southeast United States."
PLAYBOOK	WHAT Leading Activities you will do to carry out the PLAN, the SCORECARD to track those activities, and the SCRIPTS that define how you will do them	"35 Qualified Leads = > 35 Conversions = > 20 Meetings = > 15 Opportunities to Quote = > 6 POs of target size"

Figure 1.1. Example of completed roadmap, plan, and playbook for new customer acquisition

Let's illustrate further, using the example outlined in figure 1.1. Assume, for sake of argument, that the hypothetical company ("HyCo") in figure 1.1 set a one-year HOT of $7 million in revenue growth (10 percent), consisting of these revenue bridge components:

- **$0 in customer attrition**, with an ambitious goal to lose zero customers, and zero net decrease in customer volumes (pursued via an SRPP owned by the account management team, reporting to HyCo's head of sales)

- **$500,000 in price increases**, focused on a particular segment of customers and products (pursued via an SRPP owned by the account management team, reporting to HyCo's head of sales)

- **$2 million in growth from existing customers**, coming partially from selling certain customers additional products and services and partially from increased volumes to other customer segments (pursued via an SRPP owned by the outside sales team, reporting to HyCo's head of sales)

- **$3.5 million via a small acquisition** of a regional competitor, bringing a book of business and expanded footprint into a new territory (pursued via an SRPP owned by the CEO, with the assistance of others)

- **$1 million in new business** from newly acquired customers (pursued via an SRPP owned by the business development team, reporting to HyCo's head of sales)

Figure 1.1, then, outlines the specific SRPP that was developed for HyCo's last segment—$1 million in organic growth from new customer acquisition. At a high level, the roadmap assumes that HyCo's business development team will be able to acquire twenty new customers at the firm's average transaction size of $50,000 each.

It further assumes—either due to seasonality, length of sales cycles, or other sales ramp-up requirements—that twenty new customers will be acquired at a rate of two in Q1, followed by six more per quarter through the end of the year.

How many times has your sales strategy ended at the roadmap phase only to leave you disappointed when you fell short? "We need $1 million in sales—that's twenty new customers. Go!" (Or, even worse, "We need $1 million in new sales—go!") At the plan level, we avoid this, because the business development team is challenged to add specifics to your assumptions, knowing that those specifics will pull your sales strategy out of the realm of theory. HyCo sells through stocking distributors or "dealers," and the sales team has identified enough sizable prospects in the southeastern United States. They will focus on that region and put together a menu of desirable products that would help them secure an initial $50,000 stocking order from at least twenty of those dealers.

Finally, the playbook. The playbook itself consists of several subcomponents:

- Your **sales funnel** (the logic of your sales process) and the math behind each stage of that funnel (illustrated below)

- The specific **leading activities** in each stage of that funnel

- The targeted **frequency** of those leading activities, to bring opportunities further down the funnel

- How you expect the sales team to carry out those leading activities—in other words, the **script**

- The **scorecard** that you will use to (a) track the diligent completion of those activities at the specified frequencies, (b) validate the roadmap assumptions and plan specifics, (c) adjust activities in real time when necessary, and (d) hold the sales team accountable

Fortunately for HyCo, its sales funnel is straightforward, and the company has over twenty years of prior sales history to validate it. The marketing department produces qualified leads (they would have their own SRPP for that process), each of which is contacted by the salespeople as many times as necessary to hold an initial conversation. The goal of those conversations is to schedule a meeting to deliver a presentation, resulting in an opportunity to quote.

The funnel can be represented like this: HOLD CONVERSATIONS WITH QUALIFIED LEADS → DELIVER PRESENTATION AT MEETINGS → ASK FOR OPPORTUNITY TO QUOTE AND DELIVER PROPOSAL → PURCHASE ORDERS (POs) ACQUIRED. Twenty years of sales history suggests that if these activities are performed effectively, thirty-five conversations will lead to twenty meetings and fifteen quotes, enough to produce the six POs required by the roadmap.

The first three stages of the funnel are all represented as leading activities: performing the activity at each stage effectively directly leads to the next stage, and so on. "POs acquired" is a lagging outcome. You would want to know at any point in time whether the sales team is on pace to achieve that specific outcome. To do so, you could measure how many of the leading activities (e.g., conversations, presentations scheduled and delivered) they are performing compared to their targeted frequencies. You could also treat some of the leading activities as "leading indicators"—an early-warning system of sorts. In other words, if halfway through the quarter your sales team has not delivered seven or eight quotes, your desired outcome of six POs is in jeopardy. Similarly, if earlier in the quarter enough meetings have not been scheduled, you need to react right away.

To ascertain the specific direction in which you are headed, it is critical to build a clear **scorecard** for the sales team and each individual salesperson, tracking their performance at each stage (see Figure 1.2 for an example scorecard). The scorecard has two advantages. The first is accountability. Many salespeople enjoy flexibility and thrive under changing environments; it is one of the traits that make them so successful. At the same time, it can lead them to overlook or even bypass essential steps in the sales process. As an experienced sales leader once said, "Salespeople are like a river; they take the path of least resistance," which can often mean spending extra time with fewer, more receptive customers. Moreover, their innate optimism frequently leads them to believe that they will either make it all up at the end (the equivalent of a college "all-nighter" before the semester ends) or that one of their prospects will place a big enough order to make up for their failure to sign one other new account.

	METRIC	Q2 TARGET	Q1 ACTUAL QTR TO DATE
OUTCOMES	PO $ Received	$150,000,000	$500,000
	PO # Received	6	1
LEADING INDICATOR	Quotes in Pipeline	15	8
	Meetings Scheduled	20	15
LEADING ACTIVITIES	Conversions w/ Qualified Prospects	35	20
	Presentations Given	20	10

Figure 1.2. Sample scorecard for customer acquisition playbook

Without a scorecard, you lack an objective basis to ask these questions. Worse, you lack an early-warning system to identify and react to a problem in real time, while there is still time to affect the outcome. Furthermore, it is a best practice at quarterly alignment sessions to review the various scorecards as a means of holding yourselves accountable to the activities and outcomes that you committed to and to identify what the sales team needs to do more of or should be doing differently. If there is insufficient time at your annual or quarterly meeting for this exercise, we recommend a separate "sales summit" meeting.

Using a scorecard to track prespecified steps in the funnel allows salespeople to hold themselves accountable to their own optimism and keep them on pace throughout the quarter. It also offers you a "business intelligence" tool to validate the assumptions and specifics in your roadmap and plan or to offer further coaching to individual salespeople who are underperforming.

To illustrate further, the playbook should also contain a basic script that directs your salespeople on *how* each of the leading activities should be performed. The script is a guide; unless your sales department is a call center, it is not something to be memorized and recited word for word. It lays out the best practices, phrases, and arguments that effectively move the opportunity to the very next stage of the funnel. As such, it also helps your salespeople anticipate the most common questions and objections they will hear, and the most effective responses to both.

At CEO Coaching International, we prefer sales scripts inspired by Matt Dixon's classic *The Challenger Sale*. We share Dixon's premise that "every sales pitch is a conversation worth paying for." Figure 1.3 demonstrates a template for such a "challenger script" for holding a conversation with a prospect and converting it into a scheduled meeting. As you can see, the script is hardly something that is mindlessly memorized and repeated in robot-like fashion. There is ample space for the salesperson to put this in their own words. It also envisions a "data bank" of unique attention getters, teachable moments, and responses to questions or objections, which allows each pitch to be customized appropriately to the targeted prospect.

CONVERSION TO MEETING

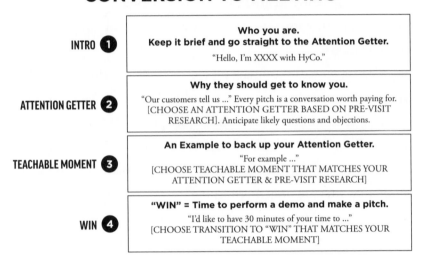

Figure 1.3. Sample sales script tool for an initial prospect conversation

Three paragraphs earlier, we referred to the scorecard as your "business intelligence tool." It is the script that provides the final piece of this BIG tool.

As you review the scorecard, you can interpret (a) what is working well that you should do more of and (b) what is going wrong and needs to be addressed. If, for example, all your salespeople are booking more meetings, converting them to quote opportunities, and closing them at a pace that is stronger than expected, you can look closely at the components of your sales strategy to figure out why and how to run up the score. However, if the company or any individual salesperson is lagging expectations, the scorecard will tell you where the most immediate problem is in real time.

Are you failing to hold enough conversations with prospects? This is easily identified and addressed. Are you failing to convert enough of those conversations to meetings, meetings to quotes, or quotes to POs? This would prompt you to address *how* those activities are being performed. The immediate response would be to audit the salesperson's delivery of the script and any supporting materials (e.g., their presentation deck at the meeting) to see if they would benefit from practice, role-playing, and coaching. If you become convinced that your salespeople are following the script, you might then call a sales meeting to discuss the effectiveness of that script and consider revisions. Are they beginning to hear questions and objections that they did not anticipate? Are the "preferred responses" to those questions and objections no longer working? Or possibly, is there something about your roadmap's assumptions and your plan's specifics that ought to be revisited?

Sometimes, while you can get far down the road to your goal via solely organic growth, the acquisition of a competitive or complementary business will certainly help achieve your goal faster. Our **Acquisition Growth Map** tool (page 247) helps you analyze the impact of one or more acquisitions on the attainment of your annual goals, often leading to BIG growth.

Thanks to the revenue bridge, sensitivity analysis, SRPP, and acquisition growth map, your team is thinking BIG. But how do you know if you can afford the investments you need to fuel your growth strategy? Enter the cash bridge analysis.

Cash Bridge

The cash bridge is designed to analyze and interpret the impact of multiple variables on your cash flow. It is used to build a strategy to extend your cash runway—the number of months of cash you have on hand—or to boost free cash flow to fund a growth initiative.

First, quantify all the various inputs that influence your change in cash from one month to the next (fixed variable expenses, accounts payable and receivable, etc.). It will produce a model to identify the triggers you need to pull to go from today's cash position to a future cash position you have identified as critical. By adjusting the variables, it will help you define the speediest path to your desired outcome. Consider creating two versions of the cash bridge: baseline and contingency. Use the different models to calculate and compare most likely, bad-news, and good-news scenarios.

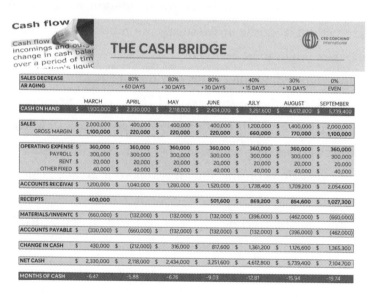

	MARCH	APRIL	MAY	JUNE	JULY	AUGUST	SEPTEMBER
SALES DECREASE		80%	80%	80%	40%	30%	0%
AR AGING		+60 DAYS	+30 DAYS	+30 DAYS	+15 DAYS	+10 DAYS	EVEN
CASH ON HAND	$ 1,900,000	$ 2,330,000	$ 2,118,000	$ 2,434,000	$ 3,251,600	$ 4,612,800	$ 5,739,400
SALES	$ 2,000,000	$ 400,000	$ 400,000	$ 400,000	$ 1,200,000	$ 1,400,000	$ 2,000,000
GROSS MARGIN	$ 1,100,000	$ 220,000	$ 220,000	$ 220,000	$ 660,000	$ 770,000	$ 1,100,000
OPERATING EXPENSE	$ 360,000	$ 360,000	$ 360,000	$ 360,000	$ 360,000	$ 360,000	$ 360,000
PAYROLL	$ 300,000	$ 300,000	$ 300,000	$ 300,000	$ 300,000	$ 300,000	$ 300,000
RENT	$ 20,000	$ 20,000	$ 20,000	$ 20,000	$ 20,000	$ 20,000	$ 20,000
OTHER FIXED	$ 40,000	$ 40,000	$ 40,000	$ 40,000	$ 40,000	$ 40,000	$ 40,000
ACCOUNTS RECEIVAI	$ 1,200,000	$ 1,040,000	$ 1,280,000	$ 1,520,000	1,738,400	$ 1,709,200	$ 2,054,600
RECEIPTS	$ 400,000			$ 501,600	$ 869,200	$ 854,600	$ 1,027,300
MATERIALS/INVENTC	$ (660,000)	$ (132,000)	$ (132,000)	$ (132,000)	$ (396,000)	$ (462,000)	$ (660,000)
ACCOUNTS PAYABLE	$ (330,000)	$ (660,000)	$ (132,000)	$ (132,000)	$ (132,000)	$ (396,000)	$ (462,000)
CHANGE IN CASH	$ 430,000	$ (212,000)	$ 316,000	817,600	$ 1,361,200	1,126,600	1,365,300
NET CASH	$ 2,330,000	$ 2,118,000	$ 2,434,000	$ 3,251,600	$ 4,612,800	$ 5,739,400	$ 7,104,700
MONTHS OF CASH	-6.47	-5.88	-6.76	-9.03	-12.81	-15.94	-19.74

Cash flow
Cash flow
incomings and ou...
change in cash balar
over a period of tim
...tion's liquid

THE CASH BRIDGE

CEO COACHING
International

The cash bridge is an important analysis that your financial team should prepare, to help you understand if you can afford the strategy you are considering—and if not, what levers you could pull to free up or raise the cash for the necessary investments.

Ensuring Success: Q1 Goals to Initiatives

Hopefully, by now you have noticed that our annual planning process differs greatly compared to the traditional "death by PowerPoint" that we have all had the misfortune to observe too frequently. Perhaps you have even experienced this in the way that you currently run your annual planning session, if you hold one at all. So far, we have stressed the importance of enabling healthy debates between your leadership team to develop a compelling, growth-centric annual business strategy using our proven framework and associated tools and analyses.

To realize your annual business strategy, you must develop a clear roadmap that depicts how the strategy will be realized over the coming year. Much like our HOT Trajectory tool helped you break down your multiyear HOT into annual goals, our **Strategic Roadmap** tool (page 251) helps you break up your annual strategy into executable quarterly themes throughout the year. Unfortunately, we often see companies declare success at the point of defining their annual goals and call the annual planning session complete. Then, the leadership team leaves the planning session and continues to do what they always have done until another planning session is called a year later and no one remembers what the annual goals were, much less having achieved any of them. Resist this urge and use our Strategic Roadmap tool to align the leadership team on quarterly themes that ensure you hit your annual goals.

Setting annual goals is the easy part. The more difficult proposition is to determine the initiatives and the specific and measurable activities that lead to achieving those outcomes. A skilled facilitator will walk you through a process that includes divergent thinking, convergent thinking, prioritizing, voting, and challenging so you arrive at a manageable number of initiatives that have a high probability of leading to achieving your goals for the year.

Here is how that works.

We want to start with determining the key company initiatives that will lead to achieving the yearly goals. These are the projects that will require the company's full organizational resources.

Begin by asking, "What *could* we do?" This process of divergent brainstorming should yield thirty to forty potential initiatives depending on the size and complexity of your company. Put the list on flip chart paper, then stick them on the wall so everybody can see them.

> A skilled facilitator will walk you through a process that includes divergent thinking, convergent thinking, prioritizing, voting, and challenging so you arrive at a manageable number of initiatives that have a high probability of leading to achieving your goals for the year.

Now ask, "What *should* we do?" We are going to converge our thinking and prioritize the top five initiatives. We come up with the top five by having each person vote for their top five. We tally the results and then look at what pops to the top. We do not stop there, and here is an example of a nuance. We will look at the top five and see if any of them are similar or can be combined with some other initiative that is out of the top five. We will also do a "challenge round" and have participants argue for why our top five may be wrong. We do not want to fall prey to groupthink.

Here are some examples of initiatives:

- Invest $25,000 per month over Q1 in new "top-of-funnel" marketing campaigns to drive at least 15 percent more qualified leads

- Topgrade 100 percent of our team and remove C players by May 1

- Hire ten new sales reps and fully ramp 80 percent of the new reps (i.e., hitting quota) by September 1

- Open a new distribution center to reduce the time to fulfill orders on the West Coast by 40 percent by the end of the year

Once we are set on the top five annual initiatives, we will assign an "owner" for each. Why an owner? Because shared ownership is no ownership. We will then have each owner lead a small group and answer the following questions for their initiative:

1. What is the most effective title for this initiative?

2. What does "success" look like when it is complete?

3. What are the big milestones or stage gates, and corresponding dates?

4. What KPIs will it impact? How will you measure it? How will this drive the outcomes we want for the year? Like we said in *MAKE BIG HAPPEN*, "If you can't define it, you can't measure it; if you can't measure it, you can't manage it."

5. What are the specific levels of support that you will require from others?

After the small groups have completed their work, we will have each owner share their answers to these questions with the full group and get feedback. Adjustments may be made and then we are set for the company-wide initiatives. Record the annual goals, initiatives, and KPIs into your **Company Dashboard** (page 253).

The Company Dashboard is the high-level tool that shows you

and everyone in your company how well the firm is performing. At a glance, you will see each key business indicator and know whether you are at, above, or below target. It should be updated and reviewed frequently by your leadership team and other key team members so everyone is aligned with what you are driving toward.

Be sure to consider a balanced scorecard approach to your dashboard. The balanced scorecard was developed by Harvard professors Robert S. Kaplan and David P. Norton in 1992.[6] The balanced scorecard allows managers to look at the business from four important perspectives:

1. Customer: How do customers see us?

    a. Customer retention

    b. Customer satisfaction

    c. Customer loyalty

    d. Market share

2. Internal business processes: What must we excel at?

    a. Product cross-sell

    b. Operational efficiency

    c. Conversion rates

    d. Decision-making

    e. Corporate culture

3. Innovation and learning: Can we continue to improve and create value?

---

6   Robert S. Kaplan and David P. Norton, "The Balanced Scorecard–Measure that Drive Performance," *Harvard Business Review Online* (January–February 1992), https://hbr.org/1992/01/the-balanced-scorecard-measures-that-drive-performance-2.

a. Training

b. Knowledge management

c. Innovation and experimentation

d. Personal growth and business goal alignment

e. Employee engagement and retention

4. Financial: How do we look to shareholders?

a. Financial results (grow revenue and EBITDA)

b. Financial efficiency (ROI, ROA, ROE)

c. Cash flow

d. Bad debt and accounts receivable management

Ten-time Inc. 5000 company Nitel is a big believer in the power of using dashboards like this. When we started working with the company, they generated $40 million in annual revenue. Ten years later, it has more than quadrupled to $175 million. One of their keys to growth was rigorously developing key metrics, tracking, and reviewing them through a dashboard and taking corrective action when results started to slip. This measurement and accountability framework works regardless of the size of your company, so there is no excuse not to implement it in your company.

Why Using a Company Dashboard Matters

- **Knowing what is happening in your business.** You know how important it is to have a window on the daily functioning of your business. But it is really hard because of the whirlwind of daily activities. You can organize the chaos through effective measurement and gain a sense of control and understanding of your business.

- **Seeing problems early.** If you measure only results, you risk missing problems that are brewing under the surface. When they finally rise to your level, corrective action will be expensive and possibly less effective. It is much better to have an accountability system in place to detect problems early while they are still small and easier to fix.

- **Finding the cause of your problems.** A good measurement system can make it easier to trace the root cause of a problem so it can be solved directly.

- **Motivating your leaders.** Accountability has extraordinary motivation effects. When people know they are accountable for their actions and results, they will put more effort in to reach them, because they know that if they do not perform, there is nowhere to hide.

- **Testing your ideas.** With the right variety of measures, you can be more open to experimentation because you can directly assess the results of your initiatives, scrap the bad ones, and expand the good ones without wasting time. If you only have one core measurement to hit, you will have less room to experiment.

- **Raising capital.** Having a top-notch measurement and account-ability system in place shows potential investors that you have your finger on the pulse of the business. With this knowledge, you can build convincing arguments for investors and banks to raise the funds you need to fund the growth of the firm.

- **Selling your business at a high premium.** Your measure-ment and accountability system could be a strategic asset of your firm and encourage buyers to pay a premium for your business. With more intimate knowledge of your business, buyers may perceive less risk and be willing to pay a high premium for your well-run firm.

To truly go from annual strategy to execution, we move right into the quarterly planning session described in MAKE BIG HAPPEN RHYTHM 3—Execute a Thirteen-Week March. With your annual strategy and goals set, the annual planning session seamlessly transitions into the quarterly alignment session for the first quarter of the year, where you get hyperfocused on execution by breaking down your annual goals and initiatives into quarterly goals and initiatives. We will talk more about the quarterly alignment session in MAKE BIG HAPPEN RHYTHM 3 later.

Recap and Next Steps

We are in the home stretch here of the annual planning session, and it is important that we take some time to recap what has been accomplished and make sure we are all in agreement.

The facilitator should recap what has been agreed to. This includes the annual goals, the company initiatives, and the KPIs. Equally important, the facilitator should memorialize the commitments that have been made by reviewing the action items captured in our **Who-What-When** tool (page 255). These are not full-blown initiatives but rather the to-do items that come out of the session. They are properly identified by continuously asking "Who will do what by when?" any time a task comes up in any meeting. A properly facilitated session will ensure that every action item has an owner and a due date.

This is also a good time to ask, "What could get in the way of achieving our plan?" Surface any issues and then assign the appropriate leader to resolve them after the meeting. By this point, there should not be any deal breakers, just friction points that need to be greased.

For next steps, set the date for the next quarterly alignment session (see MAKE BIG HAPPEN RHYTHM 3), ask each participant for their top takeaway, then take a group photo.

This can be a long one or two days. But done well, you should leave the meeting energized and with a clear roadmap to success in the year ahead.

Now let's take a moment to remind ourselves of the journey we completed:

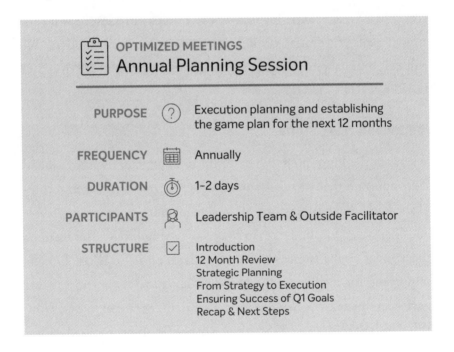

OPTIMIZED MEETINGS
Annual Planning Session

PURPOSE	?	Execution planning and establishing the game plan for the next 12 months
FREQUENCY	📅	Annually
DURATION	⏱	1-2 days
PARTICIPANTS	👤	Leadership Team & Outside Facilitator
STRUCTURE	☑	Introduction 12 Month Review Strategic Planning From Strategy to Execution Ensuring Success of Q1 Goals Recap & Next Steps

Congratulations, you have just finished the easy part. Everybody loved the annual planning session. You got to think and talk strategically. You got to put your consultant and board member hat on and work "on" the business, not "in" it. Everything is possible at this point. It is upward sloping to the right. Now comes the hard part.

How well you execute between the end of this meeting and the beginning of the next MAKE BIG HAPPEN RHYTHM determines the success or failure of your annual planning session.

Aesop figured this out 2,600 years ago when he wrote, "After all is said and done, more is said than done." Talk is cheap, but it is action that pays the bills.

Planning is 1 percent of the effort; execution is the other 99 percent. The MAKE BIG HAPPEN SYSTEM that we are walking you through ensures proper planning while setting you up for superior execution, resulting in maximum impact. Get the plan right, execute flawlessly, and bingo, you are on your way to MAKING BIG HAPPEN.

Communicate Your Plan

So, how are you, as CEO, going to build off all that momentum you and your facilitator created over the course of the planning session and MAKE BIG HAPPEN this coming year?

There are two keys to answering those questions and putting your annual plan into action. First, communicate the plan to the entire team, and second, create a culture of accountability in your organization.

Calling a company-wide meeting and sending an all-company recap video from the CEO are good places to start. The following graphic depicts a best-practices agenda for an annual company all-hands meeting, a critical communications vehicle. Share your take on the state of the industry, the state of the company, the annual goals, and the company-wide initiatives. Talk about who is responsible for what by when.

Mention your KPIs and bring them to life. Talk about how each person in the company can contribute to hitting the BIG goals and the impact that will make for them as individuals, for the company, the customers, and the community.

Employees hate feeling like they are left out of the loop. They need to know the annual plan and receive regular updates and feedback along the way on how the firm is progressing on achieving its goals and completing the initiatives.

If you are going to err, err on the side of overcommunicating, not undercommunicating.

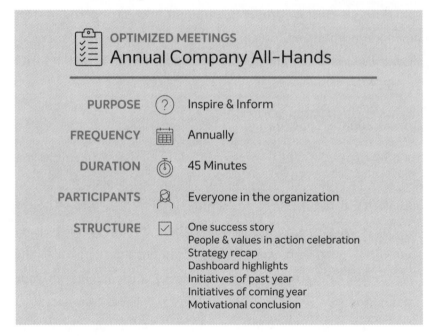

OPTIMIZED MEETINGS
Annual Company All-Hands

PURPOSE	(?)	Inspire & Inform
FREQUENCY		Annually
DURATION		45 Minutes
PARTICIPANTS		Everyone in the organization
STRUCTURE		One success story
		People & values in action celebration
		Strategy recap
		Dashboard highlights
		Initiatives of past year
		Initiatives of coming year
		Motivational conclusion

We will talk more about creating a culture of accountability in MAKE BIG HAPPEN RHYTHM 6. For now, it is time to turn your company into an execution engine through MAKE BIG HAPPEN RHYTHM 3—Execute a Thirteen-Week March.

Summary: MAKE BIG HAPPEN RHYTHM 2—Develop an Annual Plan

The annual planning session is the most important meeting of the year for you and your leadership team.

RHYTHM FREQUENCY   **ANNUALLY**

TOOL	REFERENCE
Crystal Ball	Page 237
Annual/Quarterly Planning Session Pre-Work	Page 239
Secret Ballot	Page 241
Provocative Questions	Page 243
Stop-Start-Continue	Page 245
Sales Roadmap, Plan, and Playbook	Page 249
Acquisition Growth Map	Page 247
Strategic Roadmap	Page 251
Company Dashboard	Page 253
Who-What-When	Page 255

MAKE BIG HAPPEN RHYTHM 3—Execute a Thirteen-Week March

First forget inspiration. Habit is more dependable.
Habit will sustain you whether you're inspired or not.
—*OCTAVIA BUTLER*

Thanks to your hard work in MAKE BIG HAPPEN RHYTHM 2, you now have an annual plan that the entire management team is aligned on. Finally, you are all driving the same initiatives in the same direction and starting to get movement toward your annual goals.

Unfortunately, in our experience that is where the story ends for many companies. As each leader of your executive team gets bombarded with the day-to-day challenges of their departmental roles, they quickly lose sight of the company goals and initiatives created in the annual planning session. Before you know it, the team deteriorates into reactionary firefighting only to reach the end of the year failing to hit any of the annual goals set twelve months earlier.

The antidote to this all-too-familiar scenario is to faithfully execute the annual plan according to a thirteen-week march. In fact, all our highest-performing clients, in terms of revenue and EBITDA growth, have faithfully executed a thirteen-week march, quarter after quarter and year after year.

How do you eat an elephant? One bite at a time! Done right, the goals in your annual plan represent the elephant, and the thirteen-week march breaks the goals into quarterly bite-size chunks. We do this in a quarterly alignment session, where each quarter's objectives and key activities must align with achieving the overall annual goals and initiatives that were set in the annual planning session. Essentially, what we are doing is setting annual goals, then breaking them down by quarter and saying, "What do we need to accomplish each quarter in order to make sure we are on track to hit the annual goals?"

Think of these as thirteen-week sprints. The most successful companies we coach have made the quarterly alignment session an unyielding habit, even during a pandemic. It is this healthy habit they have formed that has helped them lead their industries in growth with many achieving significant exits as a result.

> The most success-ful companies we coach have made the quarterly alignment session an unyielding habit, even during a pandemic.

CEO Coaching International partner Don Schiavone is right: success is a march. It is a systematic, deliberate quarterly process of reviewing your annual plan to determine what is working, what is not working, and what you want to do for the next thirteen weeks to keep marching toward the goals and commitments you made at your annual planning session.

Heather Nichols is a longtime CEO Coaching International client and the president of Fluid Life, a forty-plus-year family business headquartered in Edmonton, Alberta, Canada, focused on delivering equipment reliability and oil analysis services to industrial, mining, and energy clients across North America.

Long a major player in the Canadian market, Heather defined a bold vision three years ago to expand farther into the United States. Fluid Life had one US lab and a stable foothold in the market but a significantly smaller share than Heather desired and knew was possible. Naturally, a degree of internal doubt surrounded this vision, with some members of the sales and leadership teams questioning its feasibility. Unyielding, Heather confirmed her bold goal and instituted a long-term plan based on the MAKE BIG HAPPEN RHYTHMS of annual planning and quarterly thirteen-week marches. Today, US sales fuel most of her growth. Fluid Life's revenue is expanding in its home base of Canada, and they will have opened their second US location—a flagship lab in Dallas—by late summer 2021.

According to Heather, "Before we adopted the MAKE BIG HAPPEN SYSTEM, we thought we were doing an admirable job of strategic planning, meeting each year to define our goals. In retrospect, however, we never really challenged ourselves, we didn't have consistent follow-through, and we lacked a process to hold ourselves accountable. As a result, we never left our comfort zones, and we weren't really growing. Our coach at CEO Coaching International gave us a disciplined schedule and system of annual, quarterly, and weekly meetings, with tightly defined goals and initiatives represented by who/what/whens, and he helped hold us accountable to our commitments. The MAKE BIG HAPPEN SYSTEM and the outside set of eyes from our coach were key to every-thing that we've accomplished in the past three years."

Fluid Life CEO Heather Nichols

Annual Planning versus Quarterly Alignment Sessions

The quarterly alignment session shares many similarities with the annual planning session, but it gets more granular, and its focus is shorter term. Take this meeting off site and yes, use an independent, highly experienced facilitator for all the same reasons you used one for the annual planning session.

The quarterly alignment session serves several important purposes:

1. **Confirm** that the key goals and initiatives that were identified from the annual planning session are still valid.

2. **Learn** from the experiments of the previous thirteen weeks; keep the ones that worked and scrap the ones that failed.

3. **Guide** the team to create the next set of quarterly goals to achieve the annual goals.

4. Through a process of assessing and ranking, guide the participants to **narrow down** the large set of potential quarterly

initiatives to a shorter, manageable list of about five that have the highest probability of leading to achieving the annual goals and company-wide initiatives. As Jim Collins says in *Great by Choice*, fire bullets (i.e., small, calibrated experiments) that then become cannonballs (i.e., full-fledged investments).

5. **Prioritize** the agreed-upon initiatives and create a clear set of key activities, metrics, and milestones necessary to achieve each initiative.

6. **Determine** which leader is accountable for achieving each initiative and assign the cross-functional teams to deliver on each initiative.

Like the annual planning session, ask your leadership team to answer a few questions prior to this quarterly alignment session:

- What went right this quarter?

- What went wrong?

- What have we learned?

Use the quarterly alignment session also to reassess your assumptions, but do not sacrifice your annual goals except for a truly unforeseen situation. A better use of a quarterly alignment session is to look inwardly and ask what needs to change—either to stay on track to achieve your annual goals, or to get back on the right path.

Under normal circumstances, the annual goals and company-wide initiatives you set during the annual planning session would not change at a quarterly alignment session. However, the COVID-19 pandemic threw the world into a tailspin, and every business was forced to adjust its outlook or specific plans in some significant manner. By applying the framework of the quarterly alignment session to assess the impact of the pandemic on a weekly, and sometimes daily, basis, many companies were able to pivot and salvage their annual plans, and some were even able to thrive under this extraordinary generation-changing event.

Let's take a deeper look at each section of this meeting.

Quarterly Alignment Session

Similar to the annual planning session, the quarterly alignment session follows a collaborative process of reflecting on our most recent performance and assessing our current status in order to align the leadership team on the priorities for the next quarter.

Prior to the Meeting

As with the annual planning session, it is important to set up the quarterly alignment session for success with focused pre-work. This is not the time to promote death by PowerPoint. Too often when we first come into a company, we observe their quarterly planning sessions to be a multiday event where each department head feels they need to justify their existence by going into excruciating detail on every aspect of their day job via a fifty-four-page PowerPoint. One look across the room, and they realize that no one is paying attention since they are all awaiting their turn under the spotlight. While we applaud the attempt, this is not a good habit and is often hard to break.

Instead, we recommend a focused set of pre-work questions that drive at leveraging what has worked, solving what is not working, and gaining insights through learning. Our **Annual/Quarterly Alignment Session Pre-Work** (page 239) challenges the team to answer these questions and to hold one another accountable to the goals and initiatives of the previous quarter. It is accountability and realignment that form a healthy quarterly habit.

Just as you did with the annual planning session, be sure to hire a professional outside facilitator. That way the session will be led by an expert in the process, which successfully leads to meaningful outcomes, and as CEO you can be fully engaged as an active participant.

During the Meeting

Having completed the pre-work, coordinated with an off-site location to hold the meeting, and engaged a professional facilitator, you are ready to conduct the session. Here is a time-tested proven framework for success:

Introduction

Start the meeting by doing a quick check-in on how each of your leaders is doing from a personal standpoint. Great leaders care deeply about their team and do not view them as just a means to a profitable end. This check-in could take the place of a traditional icebreaker. This is also a good time to break out the **Secret Ballot** we introduced in the annual planning session to uncover any misalignment.

From there, segue into what you want to get out of today. Give a brief overview of the agenda.

At this point, take a moment and refocus everyone on the company's core values. This is a great time to reinforce the company's core values and to acknowledge and recognize the superstars in your organization who have gone above and beyond and exemplified what is best about your company. These folks might become the future leaders of your company, so take a moment to get them on your radar.

The highest-performing teams use the quarterly alignment session to make sure they have the right people doing the right things by applying our **Topgrading Exercise** (page 257) against their organization of the future. All too often we see companies struggling to hit their goal because they have outgrown the person they have in charge of the goal. By evaluating your team each quarter and aligning the skills with the needs of the company, you will set your team up for success.

Quarterly Review

Here is where we dig into the pre-meeting questions. Your facilitator will walk you through answering these questions:

- What went right this quarter?

- What went wrong?

- What have we learned?

- How did we do compared to how we said we would do on our goals?

- How did we do compared to how we said we would do on the specific and measurable activities that we are keeping score on, which we said would lead us to the outcome we wanted?

- What are our greatest opportunities in the next quarter?

- What are our greatest challenges?

- What is the number one goal we could achieve that would have the biggest impact on our growth?

At this stage of the meeting, you must push past superficial answers and keep asking questions until you get to the root causes of any shortfalls, as well as the root activities that will drive future performance. Too often, we stop the conversation at "what went wrong" and fail to identify the key leading activities that will drive future outcomes. It is like driving a car by only looking out the rearview mirror. Do not forget to look out the windshield at where you are heading. Companies that keep digging are going to find that current challenges and opportunities often reveal deeper structural inefficiencies that have been plaguing the business in less obvious ways all along.

This is also where you set a culture of accountability that starts at the top. By ruthlessly holding yourself and your leadership team accountable to the goals you set thirteen weeks ago, there is no room for excuses or hiding behind your day jobs.

It is a best practice to update and review the revenue bridge, cash bridge, and sensitivity analysis from the annual plan to see what progress we have made and what areas still need additional focus.

In times of extreme economic hardship, cash is king! To ensure you have the cash to survive, and ultimately thrive, use a Cash Bridge Dashboard to assess your runway and update it weekly until the threat is over.

Cash Bridge Dashboard

The Cash Bridge Dashboard is an early-warning system that allows you to validate the assumptions in your cash bridge in real time (recall that we introduced the cash bridge analysis as part of the annual planning process in **MAKE BIG HAPPEN RHYTHM 2** on page 64). The Cash Bridge Dashboard also offers long-term visibility into your cash flow and allows you to map out a path to the cash scenario that achieves your HOTs.

In the first column, list the key drivers of your cash bridge and leading indicators of future cash contributions. Then draw up multiple scenarios of increasing severity. Compare actual month-to-date data with those scenarios to know which scenario is in play.

Highlight variables that are meeting or exceeding the expectations of the most favorable cash bridge model in green. Indicate signs of concern and downward trends in red. This makes it easy to see which parts of your cash bridge require the most attention.

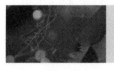 THE CASH BRIDGE **DASHBOARD**

	ACTUAL	Apr-Jun Avg SCENARIO A	July SCENARIO B	Alternative SCENARIO C
CASH ON HAND	$ 1,739,100	$ 1,700,000	$ 1,530,000	$ 1,224,000
SALES DECREASE (TREND)	-38%	-45%	-56%	-69%
BOOKINGS (TREND)	$ 292,000	$ 290,000	$ 275,000	$ 100,000
ACCOUNTS RECEIVABLE	$ 650,000	$ 530,000	$ 590,000	$ 600,000
RECEIPTS	$ 170,000	$ 230,000	$ 190,000	$ 100,000
ACCOUNTS PAYABLE	$ 90,000	$ 90,000	$ 98,000	$ 115,000
MONTHS OF CASH	3.27	3.20	2.9	2

	ACTUAL	SCENARIO A	SCENARIO B	SCENARIO C
REVENUE	$ 467,500	$ 1,700,000	$ 1,530,000	$ 1,224,000
CANADA SALARIES	$ 290,000	$ 220,000	$ 200,000	$ 150,000
US SALARIES	$ 290,000	$ 220,000	$ 200,000	$ 150,000
OTHER VARIABLE EXPENSES	$ 600,000	$ 530,000	$ 590,000	$ 590,000
ACCOUNTS RECEIVABLE	$ 120,000	$ 280,000	$ 215,000	$ 170,000
ACCOUNTS PAYABLE	$ 130,000	$ 130,000	$ 150,000	$ 180,000

Quarterly Goals and Initiatives

We know what the annual goals and company-wide initiatives are thanks to MAKE BIG HAPPEN RHYTHM 2. We know what worked and what did not work this past quarter. Now we need to take what we learned over the previous quarter and come up with new quarterly goals and initiatives that will keep us on track to hit the annual plan.

There is a direct linkage here because what happened in the prior quarter informs what we will do in the current quarter. Some goals and initiatives may carry over, some may be discarded, and we may come up with some new ones. The key is to have the courage to fail. We often see companies that learn more from their failed initiatives. It takes courage to empower a team to take risks and encourage learning through failure. If you find that you are not taking risks as a company, then you may not be setting your goals high enough. In this case, relook at our **HOT Trajectory tool** discussed in MAKE BIG HAPPEN RHYTHM 1 (core identity).

Annual goals and initiatives are big things that require tremendous effort to achieve. So how do you accomplish them? One step at a time for a total of four steps. Take your annual goals and initiatives and break them down into four steps. Then work on completing each step over the course of four quarters. This "stacking of steps" is how you get BIG things done and how you benefit from "compounding."

Here is an example. Let's say you are a US-based company and one of your annual goals is to open a new consulting office in London by the end of the year, staffed with eighty consultants who have generated a run rate of $60 million of annualized revenue by the end of the year. A big lift, right?

So, let's break it down into four quarterly initiatives and key activities. Here is what that might look like:

Q1 initiative: create consultant training program and source a list of consultant candidates.

Key activities:

- Scope out the training and determine the platform to host the training.

- Develop the training curriculum.

- Source a list of eight hundred consultants that could be a good fit for us.

Q2 initiative: hire eighty consultants and train them.

> **Key activities:**

- Narrow the sourced list of candidates down to 240 and run those 240 through a detailed interview process.

- Make offers and hire eighty.

- Start them on the training program.

Q3 initiative: sign lease for office space, create proprietary research, and promote it.

> **Key activities:**

- Secure approximately five thousand square feet of office space in the London financial district.

- Develop three proprietary research reports on topics that we consult on.

- Start promoting the research through local business press, attend three relevant conferences where we can present our research, and network with leading executives.

- Create an event for our target audience that will be delivered in Q4.

Q4 initiative: secure $60 million of annualized consulting contracts.

> **Key activities:**

- Secure twenty anchor clients with at least $1 million of annualized revenue.

- Secure seventy other clients with at least $500,000 of annualized revenue.

- Host a successful event that leads to at least $5 million in new contracts.

A BIG goal like this does not look as daunting when it is broken down into four specific and measurable steps. And since we are working in quarterly increments, we can base the next quarter's initiatives and key activities on what happened in the prior quarter.

> A BIG goal like this does not look as daunting when it is broken down into four specific and measurable steps.

The example above gave us a quarterly plan. Once you have the next quarter's goals in place, break out into small groups and ask each group to identify their top three to five quarterly initiatives to meet the next quarter's goals. Use these criteria to establish the initiatives:

1. **They must lead to achieving the corporate initiatives.** There must be a straight-line linkage between achieving your quarterly initiatives and achieving your corporate initiatives—which in turn lead to achieving your annual corporate goals.

2. **They must be significant and focused.** You have a large set of potential initiatives you could choose from. The skill in leadership is to pick the smallest number that will lead to the greatest focus and leverage in achieving your goals.

3. **They must be inspiring.** To get your team to deliver full discretionary effort, they need to be excited about the future. A well-structured objective can help.

4. **They must be specific and observable, even though they may not be measurable.** The measurable piece comes into play with the key activities that we will discuss in a moment.

The initiative is like "north." It is a direction, it is specific, and it is observable. It is about "what" you want to do and "where" you want to go.

Here are three examples of the kind of initiatives we described above:

1. Establish our firm as the leader in outsourced CFO services for SMBs.

2. Expand our franchised geographic reach into the Pacific Northwest.

3. Scale our existing reservations platform by expanding into new niches.

Now, for each of the initiatives that each group comes up with, have them develop three to five key activities and the associated KPIs. These key activities add the measurement piece to the initiatives.

An effective key activity meets these requirements:

1. **It is specific and measurable.** The key activity must be stated in such a way that at the end of the quarter you can say with 100 percent certainty that we either (a) achieved the initiative or (b) did not achieve the initiative. There is no room for "maybe" or "sort of."

2. **It supports meeting the initiative.** If each initiative were a pie, then each key activity would be one slice of the pie. Add the key activities together, and you complete the initiative.

The key activity shows you "how" you are going to measure the achievement of your initiative. Here is an example of an initiative along with three key activities that fit the framework we have been describing.

Initiative: scale our existing reservations platform by expanding into new verticals.

Key activities:

1. Identify a minimum of five verticals that could benefit from using our reservations platform.

2. Determine which verticals have at least twenty thousand potential clients for our platform.

3. Develop a pilot program with two verticals to offer our platform for free to twenty-five customers in each vertical.

4. Learn, adjust, and work out the bugs so that by the end of the quarter, we can launch an aggressive marketing campaign to attract new customers to these two verticals.

Your initiatives and key activities will help drive clarity and accountability throughout your company. It is a system that links together the disparate parts of your company, so everybody is clear on the goals and initiatives and clear on their part in achieving them.

After finally nailing down the specific and measurable initiatives that will guarantee you achieve your outcomes, you must be able to effectively communicate them to the rest of the organization. That is where our **Initiative Charter** tool (page 259) can help. As you reach alignment on each initiative during the planning session, have the executive sponsor of each initiative document the following attributes of their initiative using our initiative charter tool:

- Initiative name

- Specific and measurable outcome of the initiative (from x to y by when)

- Key activities to achieve the outcome and the lead for each activity (i.e., milestone list)

- Risks and mitigation steps for each risk

These charters serve as the starting point for MAKE BIG HAPPEN RHYTHM 6—Focus on the Outcomes. More on that later.

Once each leader has their initiative charters for the quarter in draft form, the facilitator will call everybody together and lead the group through an exercise to narrow down the initiatives and key activities. The facilitator will make sure the initiatives and key activities align with the overall company initiatives.

If you find your team struggling to identify key activities to support a particularly challenging outcome, you can use our **Leading-Lagging Indicators Sequence** tool (page 261) for a methodical way to determine the specific activities you need to engage in to achieve your initiative. Here is how it works:

With the initiatives laid out, use the tool to work backward from your goal to identify the set of specific and measurable activities required to achieve it. Your yearly or quarterly goal is what is called a *lagging indicator*. Revenue, for example, is a lagging indicator. It is the outcome of your actions, not the cause of your outcome. Lagging indicators are easy to measure but not extremely helpful in driving the growth of your business.

What we want to do is break down the drivers of the lagging indicator in a sequential chain of activities until you find the most actionable root source that you can directly influence. These activities that precede your lagging indicator are called *leading indicators*, and they are the actionable activities that you can influence, control, and directly lead to achieving your lagging indicator.

Let's say you want to increase sales. If we were coaching you on identifying your leading activities to make that happen, we might ask you questions such as these:

1. How are you going to increase sales?

2. Will growth come from new customers or existing customers?

3. If from new customers, how many new customers do you need to hit your goal and of what size?

    a. How many calls do you need to make to create a lead?

    b. How many leads turn into qualified leads, also known as opportunities?

    c. What is the conversion rate from opportunities to proposal?

    d. What is the conversion rate from initial call to booked client? How many emails do you need to send?

    e. What is the response rate on emails sent?

    f. How many are qualified?

    g. How many sales reps do you need to hire, each doing how much in sales, and what conversion rate assumptions are needed to achieve our goals?

4. If it is existing customers, how much additional revenue do you need from each customer?

    a. What additional services can you offer them?

    b. What triggers them to want to buy additional services from you?

    c. How many customer visits do you need to make?

    d. How many presentations do you need to make?

Those are just a few examples of the types of questions we might ask. Ultimately, we need to identify those initial activities that lead to achieving your goal or initiative. By doing so, you shift from emphasizing lagging indicators to driving results through execution of the leading indicators.

Whenever clients are not getting the outcomes they want, it is almost always because of a shortfall in completing the leading indicators. The **Leading-Lagging Indicators Sequence** tool helps CEOs understand how a particular outcome is generated, and if there is a shortfall, it can pinpoint where it occurred.

Execution: Focus on Top Initiatives

With our quarterly goals, initiatives, and key activities now set, we need to determine the KPIs and accountability for who is responsible for achieving each initiative.

When developing your KPIs, keep these three criteria in mind:

- Connect them to achieving your quarterly goals.

- Base them on the activities that are critical to achieving your company's success.

- Make sure they are measurable.

Here are a few examples of KPIs:

- Demos completed

- Gross profit margin

- Days sales outstanding

- Customer acquisition cost

- Monthly recurring revenue

- Click-through rate

Based on your quarterly goals, initiatives, and key activities, what KPIs make the most sense to target? Your KPIs should be a mix of leading indicators and lagging indicators and be a clear way to show your progress toward your goals and initiatives.

Once you have your quarterly KPIs identified, add them to the **Company Dashboard** you created in the annual planning session. Share it with the leadership team so everyone can readily see how you are progressing toward your quarterly goals and initiatives. Put it in a visible place so everyone can see exactly how the company is progressing on its plans. The top performers in your company want to play a game they can win. The only way they can know they are winning is if you keep score. The **Company Dashboard** helps you and your team know if they are winning or losing at any point in time. To be effective, eliminate the noise and be sure to focus on only those KPIs that you are actually trying to move through your quarterly initiatives. Anything else creates noise and focuses the team's attention on things we agreed to say no to in the planning session. This is the very definition of unfocused!

Now, we cannot forget about accountability. Just as we did in the annual planning session, somebody needs to raise their hand and say, "I've got that." Every initiative needs an owner. And every owner needs to report to the leadership team on a weekly basis—more on that in MAKE BIG HAPPEN RHYTHM 6.

Just like in the annual planning session, it is important to capture the various action items that the team identifies during the session in the form of our **Who-What-When** tool.

And like in the annual planning session, we encourage the leadership team to review their **Stop-Start-Continue** lists quarterly and hold themselves accountable to the rest of the team.

Recap and Next Steps

Conclude the meeting by summarizing the main decisions and action points by reviewing each **Initiative Charter**.

Then, review the **Who-What-When** so there is no confusion about responsibility for action items.

Finally, ask each participant to identify their top takeaways. Learn from each meeting so you can make the next meeting more effective than the prior one.

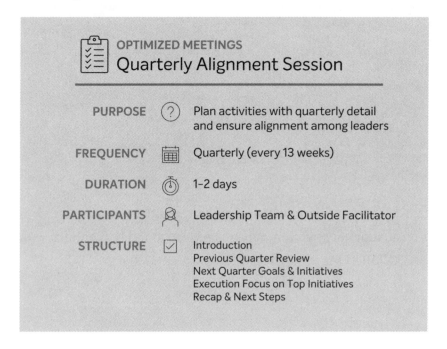

OPTIMIZED MEETINGS
Quarterly Alignment Session

PURPOSE	(?)	Plan activities with quarterly detail and ensure alignment among leaders
FREQUENCY		Quarterly (every 13 weeks)
DURATION		1-2 days
PARTICIPANTS		Leadership Team & Outside Facilitator
STRUCTURE		Introduction Previous Quarter Review Next Quarter Goals & Initiatives Execution Focus on Top Initiatives Recap & Next Steps

Communicate Your Plan

As with the annual planning session, the quarterly alignment session provides a great opportunity to communicate your quarterly plan to your team to reinforce your growth-centric culture, to provide public recognition of extraordinary efforts by team members, and to celebrate important personal milestones like birthdays and employment anniversaries. Use the quarterly company all-hands meeting agenda below as a guide for executing this important communications session.

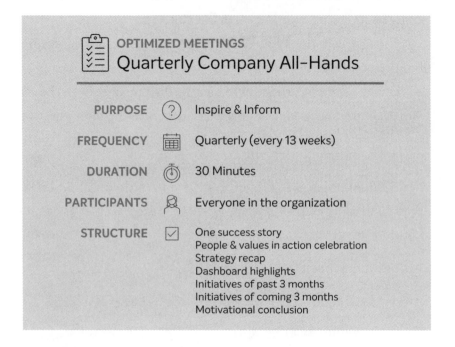

OPTIMIZED MEETINGS
Quarterly Company All-Hands

PURPOSE	(?)	Inspire & Inform
FREQUENCY		Quarterly (every 13 weeks)
DURATION		30 Minutes
PARTICIPANTS		Everyone in the organization
STRUCTURE	✓	One success story
		People & values in action celebration
		Strategy recap
		Dashboard highlights
		Initiatives of past 3 months
		Initiatives of coming 3 months
		Motivational conclusion

With quarterly initiatives and key activities now in place, it is time to shift our attention from quarterly to monthly alignment with MAKE BIG HAPPEN RHYTHM 4—Stay on Track.

Summary: MAKE BIG HAPPEN RHYTHM 3—Execute a Thirteen-Week March

The thirteen-week march centers around the quarterly alignment session, where you achieve your annual goals through the habit of quarterly realignment and accountability.

RHYTHM FREQUENCY — **QUARTERLY**

TOOL	REFERENCE
Annual/Quarterly Alignment Session Pre-Work	Page 239
Secret Ballot	Page 241
Topgrading Exercise	Page 257
Initiative Charter	Page 259
Leading-Lagging Indicators Sequence	Page 261
Company Dashboard	Page 253
Who-What-When	Page 255
Stop-Start-Continue	Page 245

MAKE BIG HAPPEN RHYTHM 4—Stay on Track

Our greatest weakness lies in giving up. The most certain
way to succeed is always to try just one more time.
—*THOMAS EDISON*

Jamil Nizam of Waldom Electronics is one CEO who has earned the benefits of having the discipline of an outcomes-oriented monthly rhythm. Loyal to the annual and quarterly MAKE BIG HAPPEN RHYTHMS of planning and accountability for six consecutive years, Waldom has enjoyed consistent year-over-year growth. Recognizing there might be more opportunity to take the company to the next level, Jamil decided to establish our strategic assessment, as we will describe shortly.

A global nine-figure company, the Waldom team recently began holding a separate strategic assessment meeting with the North America, EMEA, and APAC regions to review the progress of their quarterly initiatives. By keeping several different business units on a tighter track, the monthly cadence launched the company into the most outsized results they have ever experienced: 20 percent growth in revenue and 80 percent growth in EBITDA in their most recent quarter alone.

Waldom executive leadership team in a planning session

If you made it this far, you now have an annual plan that defines a strategy to execute on your core identity on your way to your HOT, a detailed quarterly plan based on specific and measurable outcomes, and a focused set of initiatives to achieve the quarterly outcomes.

If done well, the quarterly plan will also include one or two experiments that have the biggest potential to move your growth drivers, as determined by your sensitivity analysis.

Do not celebrate yet! Thirteen weeks is a long time. A lot can happen between quarterly alignment sessions that could impact your quarterly plans. The best-performing firms understand that plans change the minute after they are published and have a healthy monthly rhythm to review the events of the past month and systematically assess these changes against the plans, making incremental adjustments as needed.

We often see test results from an experiment ran with high hopes of it being the home run for the year and then come back with unintended consequences causing the cancellation of the experiment altogether.

Setbacks like this can make you and your team want to give up and go back into firefighting mode. However, reactionary leadership puts an emphasis on activity. The MAKE BIG HAPPEN RHYTHMS are focused on proactive leadership with an emphasis on outcomes.

> **Only activities directed at outcomes truly matter.**

This is an essential difference since activity for activity's sake is pointless. Only activities directed at **outcomes** truly matter.

All too often we go into businesses that have spent enormous energy crafting detailed annual and/or quarterly plans, only to see them shelved soon after inception with no way to make course adjustments along the journey.

This is where the monthly MAKE BIG HAPPEN RHYTHM 4 helps you stay on track. It is centered on two key alignment meetings:

1. Financial performance review—understand the financial health of the business and spot any trends.

2. Strategic assessment—proactively challenge the strategy we set for the quarter and make incremental changes as warranted.

Financial Performance Review

It is surprising to us how often we start working with a firm to find out they do not have any formal review of their financial performance until they start collecting data for their tax return each spring. To be fair, most leaders in this situation state that they look at their financial performance every day, so why add another review?

However, tracking your favorite financial metrics daily is not the same as digging into the overall health of your business every month based on an official close of your accounting books.

If you do not have an accountant or a bookkeeper, then get one! Consider starting with a fractional accounting and/or CFO firm that can properly close your books each month and generate department-level monthly budgets. This information is critical to managing a high-growth business. Without it, you are flying blind. The first step is to make sure you have the financial talent to provide you with quality financial statements and budgets each month. You are looking for a monthly comparison of actuals to budget and a full set of financial statements (balance sheet, profit and loss, and cash flow), and in times when cash is tight, be sure to dust off the Cash Bridge Dashboard analysis discussed in the previous MAKE BIG HAPPEN RHYTHMS so you have a real-time understanding of your cash runway.

Now that you have a monthly budget and financial statement to review, it is time to set aside the time to review them in earnest. We realize not every leader has an MBA or a deep finance background. Do not let this be your excuse to shy away. Instead, use our **Monthly Financial Review Checklist** (page 263) to help you ask the right questions of your finance team and understand the true health of your business.

A healthy financial review includes an understanding of key trends in your financial performance. We recommend looking at the following financial indicators on a rolling twelve-month graph to spot trends and take corrective action:

- Revenue

- Gross margin

- COGS

- Cost of acquiring a customer

- Operating expenses by department

- Net margin

- Efficiency metrics unique to your business (e.g., utilization rates, revenue per employee, leads, conversion rate, average revenue per client, churn, capacity utilization, asset turnover)

Healthy budget hygiene is also essential. Do you understand every driver that caused an expense account to go over budget? How will this expense overage be corrected? Do other expense categories get cut to ensure a balanced budget going forward? If not, how does that flow through to your quarterly initiatives and KPIs? How will you deploy any budget surpluses? This might be the opportunity to take a budget surplus from one category and redeploy it to a quarterly experiment that is showing promise.

As you answer the questions coming out of your monthly financial review, be sure to update the **Who-What-When** tracker so nothing falls through the cracks.

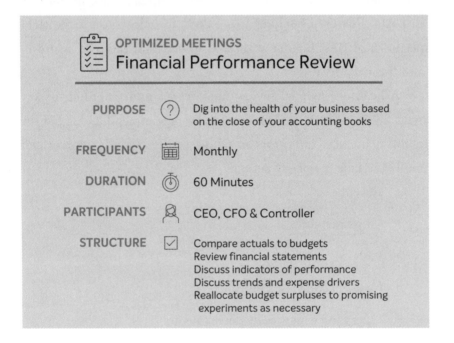

OPTIMIZED MEETINGS
Financial Performance Review

PURPOSE	(?)	Dig into the health of your business based on the close of your accounting books
FREQUENCY		Monthly
DURATION		60 Minutes
PARTICIPANTS		CEO, CFO & Controller
STRUCTURE		Compare actuals to budgets Review financial statements Discuss indicators of performance Discuss trends and expense drivers Reallocate budget surpluses to promising experiments as necessary

CEO Coaching International partner Tracy Tolbert spent a large part of his career in management at ACS, a publicly traded *Fortune* 500 company later acquired by Xerox. "The senior business leaders at ACS managed the company through monthly financial reporting," Tracy shared. "As a multibillion-dollar company, we had to stay very close to the numbers to continue to grow. The monthly financial performance review was integral to our success."

Because ACS had several large divisions, anyone in the company who owned a profit and loss statement participated in the meeting, along with the CEO, COO, CFO, and head of sales. In the review, they would compare the last month's financials not only against their original plan but also against the same period in the previous year.

This level of analysis may not be necessary in your company. As you implement a monthly financial performance review, set its content to cover the most important metrics in your business and adjust the format to fit your business's needs. No matter what, do not skip this rhythm. In Tracy's words, "Reviewing finances each month is critical in every single business."

Monthly Strategic Review

We have a saying: "Hope is not a strategy." While we hope our plans will work out, there are way too many variables in operating a successful business to ensure we can get it all right at the beginning of each quarter.

Every day has the potential to identify new opportunities or uncover new challenges. As you learn from your successes and your failures, you must build in the time to stop and reflect. Are the strategies we set in our annual and/or quarterly planning sessions still valid? How do the results from the latest experiment affect our plans? How will the unexpected departure of a critical leader affect the team and their KPIs? How will the merger of my two largest suppliers affect my supply chain?

Take the time after your monthly financial performance review to ask your leadership team questions like the ones above. While the right questions to ask are obvious in times of trouble, the leading growth-centric companies challenge themselves to ask these kinds of tough questions even when things are seemingly going well.

Start by reviewing the **Company Dashboard** with your leadership team by using a questioning mindset to spot any trends in the KPIs. This is not a rehash of the day-to-day battles. We will cover that in MAKE BIG HAPPEN RHYTHM 5. Instead, focus on the trends and what they may or may not say about our previously defined strategies and tactics. Use the monthly strategic review agenda below to ensure the plans you made are still valid and to get in front of any strategic adjustments that may be needed.

All too often we see leadership teams scrap their entire plans for the year at the first bump in the road. Do not give up! Usually, the root of the challenge requires minor changes to strategies and/or tactics. Take a breath, and pressure test your strategies against your tactics in this monthly business rhythm.

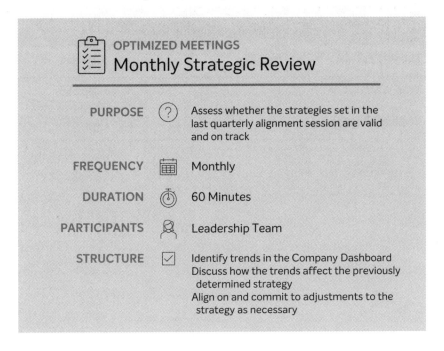

OPTIMIZED MEETINGS
Monthly Strategic Review

PURPOSE (?) Assess whether the strategies set in the last quarterly alignment session are valid and on track

FREQUENCY Monthly

DURATION 60 Minutes

PARTICIPANTS Leadership Team

STRUCTURE Identify trends in the Company Dashboard
Discuss how the trends affect the previously determined strategy
Align on and commit to adjustments to the strategy as necessary

Summary: MAKE BIG HAPPEN
RHYTHM 4—Stay on Track

Stay on track by including a monthly rhythm of financial and strategic reviews with your leadership team.

RHYTHM FREQUENCY **MONTHLY**

TOOL	REFERENCE
Monthly Financial Review Checklist	Page 263
Who-What-When	Page 255
Company Dashboard	Page 253

MAKE BIG HAPPEN RHYTHM 5—Hold Yourself Accountable

Accountability breeds response-ability.
—STEPHEN R. COVEY

Ultimately, we are in business to accomplish something. We want to deliver a great product or outstanding service to our clients. We want to build something of lasting value. We want to do well by our team members and our community. And yes, we want to make a good profit. Now, none of those things happen on their own. You must create an environment—a culture—that fosters, recognizes, and rewards the behaviors that lead to the goals and results you are trying to achieve.

To recognize and reward those behaviors, you must track and measure the results. You cannot hold people accountable unless you clearly, diligently, and religiously measure what you and others are doing toward the attainment of your goals. Without measurement there can be no management.

By following the first four MAKE BIG HAPPEN RHYTHMS, you have made great strides in setting your team up for success and are in a much better position to hold them accountable. Properly implemented, the MAKE BIG HAPPEN SYSTEM has thus far provided you with a clear vision, a HOT to make the vision a reality, an annual strategic plan to align the leadership team, a healthy financial foundation to continue to build upon, and a focused set of quarterly goals and initiatives to drive growth.

MAKE BIG HAPPEN RHYTHM 5 is a bimonthly rhythm focused on holding the CEO and the rest of the management team accountable to the process and the outcomes. It is driven by bimonthly accountability sessions.

Having a twice-per-month, one-on-one session with an accountability partner is an essential yet often overlooked business rhythm. This is the venue for the CEO and their key executives to be held accountable by an outside third party.

These are distinct from other forms of personal accountability we see companies implement. First, the bimonthly accountability session is conducted with someone outside the organization and its day-to-day distractions and possibly its own tunnel vision. At CEO Coaching International, we fulfill this role with several hundred CEOs and their leadership teams. Accountability is a foundational trait of a world-class business coach. Second, these sessions allow for in-depth diagnostics around what is going right or wrong with the plan, how to overcome unexpected obstacles, and a detailed set of commitments to make progress week to week. Third, they allow a forum to neutralize curveballs and shiny objects that might otherwise distract you.

The format of the bimonthly accountability session is very straightforward:

- Review metrics related to the activities and outcomes behind your quarterly, annual, and long-term HOTs.

- Review commitments made in the last accountability meeting. How did you do on those commitments? Did they have an impact? How do you know?

- Did any new topics arise that affect your quarterly, annual, and long-term HOTs?

- Based on this discussion, what are the new commitments that you will make and complete between now and your next meeting?

At these sessions, the circumstances may call upon you to select one of the MAKE BIG HAPPEN TOOLS covered in chapter 3. Some of these tools might be reviewed during the session, or perhaps the results from the tool(s) create a "new commitment" for discussion at the next session.

In our experience coaching hundreds of firms across the world, those management teams that commit to regular accountability sessions consistently outperform their peers.

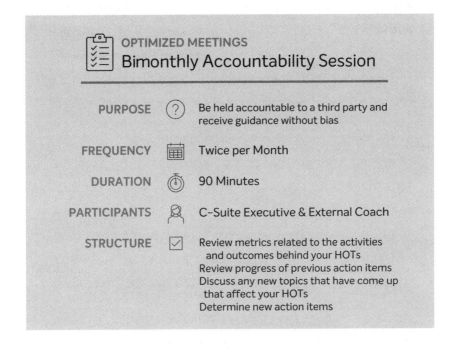

OPTIMIZED MEETINGS
Bimonthly Accountability Session

PURPOSE	?	Be held accountable to a third party and receive guidance without bias
FREQUENCY		Twice per Month
DURATION		90 Minutes
PARTICIPANTS		C–Suite Executive & External Coach
STRUCTURE	☑	Review metrics related to the activities and outcomes behind your HOTs
Review progress of previous action items
Discuss any new topics that have come up that affect your HOTs
Determine new action items

Jan Bednar is the founder and CEO of one of the world's fastest-growing logistics providers, as well as a member of the elite *Forbes* 30 Under 30 club. His company, ShipMonk, specializes in helping e-commerce businesses scale through world-class supply chain management and order fulfillment.

In February of 2020, ShipMonk was on a high-growth trajectory. Jan, an analytical visionary, had his hands full with directing operations, hiring new employees, oversee-ing the sales process, and negotiating important deals. As the leader of a company on a rocket-powered path, these demands were expected, but not the easiest to shoulder.

To help manage ShipMonk's expansion, Jan engaged CEO Coaching International and began to work through the four Make BIG Happen questions. They talked through risks, how to problem-solve in the short term, and how to negotiate the best value for his aforementioned deal. Then came March of 2020. Like the rest of the world, Jan's plans for the future pivoted 180 degrees overnight.

As an e-commerce company reliant on shipping carriers, warehouse workers, and the global supply chain, ShipMonk was faced with some formidable roadblocks. With retail locations rendered mostly inaccessible, customers flocked to online shopping. As a result, incredible pressure was placed on existing infrastructures, which were not ready to handle such an explosive increase in order volume.

COVID-19 had the potential to stop ShipMonk in its tracks,

but Jan stayed true to his mission and continued with his bimonthly accountability sessions. He bounced ideas off his coach, who, in turn, helped him take advantage of the Make BIG Happen questions. With a sounding board that had been there and done that, Jan was able to gain the confidence he needed to make important decisions throughout the pandemic. With an experienced accountability partner by his side, it was impossible to be lonely at the top.

With the assistance of his coach and his biweekly check-ins, Jan had weathered a storm that could've caused some serious damage otherwise. In December of 2020, amid the chaos of Black Friday and Cyber Monday, ShipMonk secured $290 million in growth equity funding from Summit Partners. Just a month later, they received an additional $65 million from Periphas Capital, thus ending commerce's most exigent year on a resoundingly positive note.

CEO Jan Bednar enjoys some fun in the office knowing his company, ShipMonk, has more than doubled its order volume, customer base, and annual revenue since 2020.

By maintaining bimonthly accountability meetings, you, too, can navigate your company's challenges of any magnitude.

Summary: MAKE BIG HAPPEN RHYTHM 5—Hold Yourself Accountable

Are you ready to take your accountability to a whole new level?

RHYTHM FREQUENCY	BIMONTHLY (TWICE A MONTH)

TOOL	REFERENCE
As assigned by your coach	Part II, chapter 3

MAKE BIG HAPPEN RHYTHM 6—Focus on the Outcomes

Don't mistake activity with achievement.
—JOHN WOODEN

One of the biggest impacts you can make to your growth trajectory is to enable your entire team, at every level of the organization, to adopt a test mindset. All too often, we come into an organization that is led from the top down with tight controls to ensure the team does what they are told.

The fallacy in this leadership technique is that your company will only be as successful as the ideas generated at the top. However, if you look at the fastest-growing companies, you will quickly find that the ideas that are driving the growth are coming from the trenches. We are not talking about home run ideas that propel the company in a whole new direction. Instead, we are talking about the day-by-day incremental improvements coming from all levels of the organization and from all departments that add up to tremendous change over the year.

How do you instill this mindset?

You must engage the team by giving them autonomy. In the book *Drive*, author Dan Pink shows how top performers come prewired with high motivation. Our job as leaders is to harness this motivation by giving them the autonomy to apply their skills to tackle problems with a purpose. In practical terms, this means stop assigning your teams tasks to accomplish. If you and

> If you look at the fastest-growing companies, you will quickly find that the ideas that are driving the growth are coming from the trenches.

your leadership team have already broken down a challenge into the lowest-level tasks to perform, then there is little challenge left for your top performers to get excited about and to leverage their skills.

Instead, focus on the outcomes you defined in your quarterly alignment session. These are the lagging indicators of success that you and your leadership team have aligned on as the most important goals of the quarter. By providing clarity on a focused set of outcomes to achieve in a finite time frame (i.e., by the end of the quarter), we are setting up the team to play a game they can win. The definition of a successful game the team can win starts with the **Initiative Charter**, introduced in MAKE BIG HAPPEN RHYTHM 3—Thirteen-Week March. It is in the initiative charter where you defined the specific and measurable outcome(s) of the initiative, defined the cross-functional team to work the initiative, identified the obvious risks, and put together risk mitigation plans.

One mistake leadership teams often make in the quarterly alignment session is to put too much detail into the initiative charter. It is a charter, not a detailed step-by-step plan. If you are challenging yourselves properly during the quarterly alignment sessions, then your quarterly goals, and hence the respective initiatives that drive each goal, require a cross-functional team to drive new capabilities that did not exist before. Otherwise, you are defining departmental projects that should be assigned to the department leader rather than wasting the time of the entire leadership team.

It is a delicate balance of providing enough clarity to the team to align them on the outcome (i.e., goal) and enough autonomy to enable them to leverage their unique skills and understanding of the business from their viewpoint. Often, this involves allowing each team that owns a quarterly initiative some freedom to experiment, or, as Jim Collins calls it, "fire a bullet." For it is in these experiments, whether they succeed or fail, where the biggest impact to your company's growth trajectory will occur.

Weekly Move-the-Needle Sessions

So how do you encourage freedom to experiment yet hold the teams accountable to their outcomes?

The answer lies in a weekly business rhythm we call the Move-the-Needle (MTN) session. This is where the cross-functional team meets to test their hypothesis on leading indicators and move the needle on the goal (i.e., outcome/lagging indicator). The participants in an MTN session are the key players responsible for taking the initiative over the finish line, regardless of their level in the org chart or which department they are from. We will cover weekly departmental meetings in the next section.

There is a separate weekly MTN session for every quarterly initiative. This is a down and dirty session with the team that owns the initiative—and they only discuss the initiative, period! Your first chance of success starts by identifying the right cross-functional team during or right after the quarterly alignment session. Yes, there is an executive sponsor from the leadership team who "owns" the initiative. *No*, the executive sponsor is not responsible for doing all the work. In fact, more often than not they empower the underlying team to do all the work. The executive sponsor's main role is to ensure that the MTN session happens each week, that each team member updates the **Initiative Commitments Tracker** (page 267) prior to the meeting, and that the **Goal Scoreboard** (page 265) is updated before each session.

During the MTN session, each team member reviews the following:

1. The actions they committed to take since the last session

2. The impact these actions had on the leading indicator(s)

3. If they failed to take their committed action, the root cause and how they will overcome it in the future

4. Actions they will commit to take over the coming week to move the needle of the leading indicator(s)

That is it! It sounds simple, but it takes practice and a commitment to doing only those activities that have a high probability of affecting the outcome. This is in stark contrast to many organizations that value raw activity output and have no idea if they are moving the growth needle.

During the MTN session, the executive sponsor assesses the collective actions of the entire team by reviewing any movement in the leading indicators and, more importantly, any respective movement in the outcome via the **Goal Scoreboard**.

It is the team's responsibility to work the leading indicators of the initiative and then track definitively whether the change in the leading indicator is making an impact to the outcome. Our **Goal Scoreboard** tool helps the team keep score for their initiative. This is a highly specific scoreboard for the initiative that must track the daily/weekly/monthly trends in the leading indicator against the respective changes in the outcome. Remember to encourage some actions by the team to be true experiments that can fail. Through failure, the team will develop an even deeper understanding of the unit economics of the business and how their actions may or may not affect them.

The **Goal Scoreboard** is not to be confused with the **Company Dashboard**, which was discussed in MAKE BIG HAPPEN RHYTHMS 2, 3, and 4. The Company Dashboard is a summary-level dashboard of the company's goals, initiatives, and KPIs. It will report on the monthly changes to quarterly goals and initiatives and is used by the entire company to know what the score is for the firm.

The Goal Scoreboard is primarily used, however, by the team assigned to the initiative(s) impacting the goal. It enables the team to understand what drivers (i.e., leading indicators) truly move the needle of the outcome. The most effective Goal Scoreboards are updated much more often than monthly. The team needs to be able to see how their daily efforts impact the score. Herein lies the biggest challenge. Most outcomes are difficult to measure and the leading indicators that will truly move the needle are even harder still to measure. The leadership team must consider this dilemma when defining the initiative in the quarterly alignment session. Often, the first phase of the initiative entails developing new processes, tools, and measurements to properly measure the outcomes and their associated leading indicators.

For example, we had a client that relied on a direct sales model to grow revenue. From the high-level financials, we could see that some sales reps sold more than others. However, we lacked visibility into conversion rate by rep. After probing during a quarterly alignment session, it became clear that the company had no way to track the distribution of leads to each rep coming from their marketing engine. That was because their marketing engine had a call to action to the firm's global phone number, where the first rep to pick up the call got the lead. After repeated attempts to try to enforce call logging into their CRM to capture lead assignments, the team realized they needed to create a new initiative that would automate the distribution of phone leads, which required an entirely new phone system. So, the selection and implementation of a new phone system became the new quarterly initiative to support the capture of critical leading indicators to drive revenue growth.

The point of this example is to encourage you to do the hard work of capturing the measurements you need to drive growth. Rather than use the lack of data as an excuse for inaction, take the first step and create a cross-functional team to go get the data, no matter how hard it may seem initially.

Go empower your cross-functional teams to MAKE BIG HAPPEN through a weekly focus on the most important outcomes driving the growth of your business.

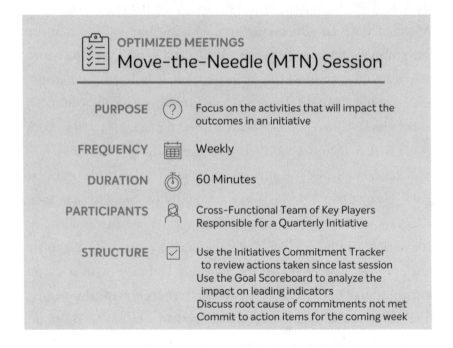

OPTIMIZED MEETINGS
Move-the-Needle (MTN) Session

PURPOSE	Focus on the activities that will impact the outcomes in an initiative
FREQUENCY	Weekly
DURATION	60 Minutes
PARTICIPANTS	Cross-Functional Team of Key Players Responsible for a Quarterly Initiative
STRUCTURE	Use the Initiatives Commitment Tracker to review actions taken since last session Use the Goal Scoreboard to analyze the impact on leading indicators Discuss root cause of commitments not met Commit to action items for the coming week

Before he was twenty-five, Victor Santos, a standout fintech entrepreneur, had founded Airfox with a vision to bring digital banking tools to accelerate financial inclusion in emerging markets, including Brazil. Victor was passionate about the prospect of providing banking services to those lacking resources in Latin American countries. A brilliant and fearless mind, he had passion, commitment, and a strong belief in making a meaningful impact on the world.

For Victor, forming an inspirational vision of the future was easy, but managing a rapidly growing operations team for the first time was not a walk in the park. With a deluge of downloads in what felt like overnight, the new CEO needed to invest in software development to keep up with high growth. A huge opportunity arose to partner with Via Varejo, one of the most well-known multinational megaretailers. On top of that, he had to manage funding, potential cryptocurrency deals, and a rebrand of the digitally inclusive Brazilian neo bank app to banQi.

Who has time to implement healthy business rhythms with a to-do list that long?

Amid the whirlwind of the day-to-day, Victor decided to adopt the MAKE BIG HAPPEN SYSTEM. As he hustled throughout each week to manage key relationships with boards and investors, weekly leadership team meetings helped him and his team consistently stop and ensure that the company was progressing week-over-week in the right direction.

"We struggled with implementing OKRs prior to the MAKE BIG HAPPEN SYSTEM," says Santos. "We overengineered the system at first. There was a lot of trickling down of the OKRs in the company. I had this tendency, as many founders do, of trying to solve every problem. My coach helped keep me honest and understand my pain points, strengths, and weaknesses. I learned how to let my team lead and give them clear instructions on where we are going but make sure they understood they had ownership and let them figure out the 'how.' That was a huge mindset shift for me, which paid off. After implementing the MAKE BIG HAPPEN SYSTEM, we went from 50 percent completion of our OKRs to over 90 percent."

Through their Move-the-Needle sessions, Victor and his team focused in on the KPIs of their quarterly initiatives. Victor knew that to successfully navigate the business's growth amid the realities of their unstable market, constant testing and micropivoting were necessary. So, on a weekly basis, Victor and the Airfox team focused in on the specific and measurable activities they needed to execute on to achieve their HOTs.

"We only had three goals in a quarter and spent a day with our coach to reverse engineer how we got to those goals. The session was very efficient. There was never one second where we did not feel like we were making progress somehow. We came out of it with so much alignment and clarity," Victor shared. "It was about more than just the awareness too. We were also able to figure out how we implement what we've agreed to. I had a weekly meeting with my management team that originally was super open ended. People would just talk. It was a meeting that should have been an email. I am a little bit disorganized, and my brain would jump all over the place. I needed someone to give me a rigorous agenda and be more purposeful with the meetings. We followed the MAKE BIG HAPPEN template and got extremely helpful feedback from our coach. He really helped us see how to go from a plan for the whole year all the way down to what to do every day."

For a CEO in Victor's position, managing a multimillion-dollar company with the soul of a scrappy start-up and a desire to sell, stress was inevitable, and failure was likely. Despite all odds, in May 2020, Airfox had a successful sale to Brazilian multinational retail giant Via Varejo for a jaw-dropping valuation. Revenue had grown thirteen times in one year—in just eighteen months the company exploded from one thousand active transacting users to five hundred thousand.

Commenting on his coach, Victor shared, "Some days he was a sounding board, sometimes a therapist, sometimes a doctor diagnosing what's wrong. There must be impression management with your board, and sometimes you do not get the whole truth from your own management team, so he has been the person where I could vomit everything that was on my mind. Get out of my own way by seeing if I had a bias to break through. He coached other members of my team, too, was able to see both perspectives, keep the confidentiality, and always do what is rationally the best thing for the company."

CEO Victor Santos (standing with arms crossed at center) surrounded by Airfox team members

Weekly Leadership Meeting

While your weekly MTN sessions are all about laying new track (i.e., achieving quarterly goals that enable new levels of performance), it is in your weekly leadership team meeting where the entire executive team ensures the trains are running on time (i.e., department-level accountability). The weekly leadership meeting is a regular, nonnegotiable critical link in the MAKE BIG HAPPEN SYSTEM and ensures that you and your leadership team are collaborating, making progress, and surmounting any obstacles that might be getting in their way in their "day jobs." It is key for these meetings to be consistent: schedule them for the same day and time each week.

The weekly leadership meeting focuses on reviewing weekly tactical progress of the company. You will also review the **Company Dashboard** (discussed in MAKE BIG HAPPEN RHYTHMS 2, 3, and 4) containing your key performance indicators (KPIs).

We use a structured four-part weekly leadership meeting format that covers results, progress, issues, and discussion, or "RPID" for short (pronounced "rapid"). This meeting, which can be done in sixty minutes, forces you to stay on point, holds people accountable to results, and leaves room to discuss and resolve issues that are getting in the way. The four parts of RPID are as follows:

1. **Results.** A ten-minute review of the **Company Dashboard** that tracks the metrics that are most critical to your company's success. Make sure everyone understands where your numbers are and where they should be. While a good company dashboard will show if we are down 5 percent or up 15 percent, etc., the real questions are "Why?" and "What action do we need to take?" Answering these questions requires analysis that the team member needs to do before the meeting and then share at the meeting to drive meaningful discussion.

2. **Progress.** Give each leader two or three minutes max to report on how their department is doing in moving these key metrics forward. Do not let your leaders recite their to-do lists or turn these into twenty-minute monologues. You only want to focus on the progress being made on the leading activities that will lead you to the outcomes you want.

3. **Issues.** Go around the room and ask each leader if they have any issues that need to be addressed. You want to surface obstacles that are or could get in the way of achieving your

quarterly goals. Keep this part of the meeting moving by acknowledging the issue and then moving on to the next issue. We are building an action list here, not solving all the company's problems.

4. **Discussion.** After every leader has raised their issues, select one or two pressing concerns that are directly related to progress on KPIs. It is the CEO's, managing director's, or leader's responsibility to keep the discussion focused on just these topics. A supply chain issue that might cripple this month's numbers needs to be talked out. A cool new piece of tech that could streamline your supply chain next year does not. Determine next steps to resolve the key issues and who is responsible for handling them. Make sure you have a follow-up system to ensure the issue gets resolved. Finish this part by asking if anyone on the team needs help from someone else on the team or to solve an issue that was not discussed here. Then make plans to discuss that at a different meeting.

Use the RPID framework to do this, and you will be well on your way to BIG results.

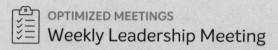

OPTIMIZED MEETINGS
Weekly Leadership Meeting

PURPOSE		Ensure the team is collaborating, making progress and surmounting any obstacles
FREQUENCY		Weekly
DURATION		60 Minutes
PARTICIPANTS		Leadership Team
STRUCTURE		**RPID:** Results Progress Issues Discussion

When one particular CEO reached out to us for coaching in 2018, his company was making $12 million in annual revenue and had a goal to sell for $40 million. At the time, his business had no rhythms, no planning methods, no differentiation between activity and achievement. To understand the lay of the land at the company, his coach sent out a survey asking the leadership team how many hours per week they were spending in meetings, and the cumulative total was 144 hours. The CEO recognized there was a lot of room for improvement in their efficiency and fully adopted the MAKE BIG HAPPEN SYSTEM. The CEO and his team implemented our weekly meeting format, making his leadership meetings metric-based, focused on leading activities, and glaringly more purposeful.

After some time, the client's coach sent out the survey again, and with the same number of team members the amount of time spent in meetings had reduced to 41 hours. The team not only enjoys the day-to-day of their job immeasurably more, but their use of the system has also allowed them to achieve growth they never dreamed of. In April 2021, the CEO and his team sold a portion of the business based on a valuation of $122 million, over three times greater than the goal they had just two years earlier.

Weekly Departmental Team Meetings

To be a growth leader, you will want to push accountability down the organization beyond the leadership team. Each member of your leadership team should hold a similar meeting every week with their own direct reports, preferably a day or two prior to your weekly leadership meeting. This accomplishes three important things. First, it allows your senior executive to arm themselves with the latest updates for your weekly leadership meeting. Second, it helps your senior executive hold their team accountable for following through on the quarterly goals, initiatives, and key activities. Third, it is a great communication mechanism to ensure lower levels of the organization are getting real-time updates on the company's progress.

Weekly One-on-Ones

Thus far, we have been talking about team accountability since business is a team sport. However, an often-overlooked opportunity for two-way personal accountability is in the weekly one-on-one.

We encourage anyone that has direct supervision over another employee to conduct a weekly one-on-one with each team member. This session enables you as a leader to develop true empathy with your employees. People do not work for companies. They work for people. The stronger the relationship you have with your employees, the stronger their bond to the company.

> The stronger the relationship you have with your employees, the stronger their bond to the company.

An effective one-on-one has three parts:

- **Stop-Start-Continue**—open the session by focusing on them. Our **Stop-Start-Continue** tool (page 245) enables you to gain valuable feedback on what you and the company are doing well and what could use improvement.

- **Personal development**—focus this time on the personal goals you have for them. There is plenty of time in the previous five MAKE BIG HAPPEN RHYTHMS to challenge them on their team goals. Instead, resist the urge for yet another goal check-in session by focusing on their personal development. What skills, training, or support do they need to master their current role? Show that you care to help them become the best versions of themselves.

- **Career development**—as they grow their personal skills, help them understand where they could go within your organization and help them build the skills to get there.

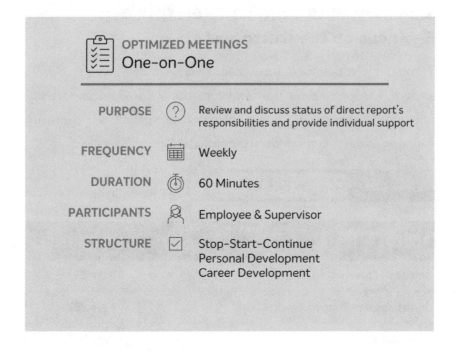

By investing in your team through weekly one-on-ones, you will supercharge your key growth engine: your team!

Summary: MAKE BIG HAPPEN RHYTHM 6—Focus on the Outcomes

Through a relentless focus on outcomes via a weekly Move-the-Needle session, weekly leadership team and departmental sessions, and weekly one-on-ones, your teams will be better engaged, and your company will unlock the potential for hypergrowth.

RHYTHM FREQUENCY **WEEKLY**

TOOL	REFERENCE
Initiative Charter	Page 259
Initiative Commitments Tracker	Page 267
Goal Scoreboard	Page 265
Company Dashboard	Page 253
Stop-Start-Continue	Page 245

MAKE BIG HAPPEN RHYTHM 7—Increase Productivity

What you do makes a difference, and you have to decide
what kind of difference you want to make.
—*JANE GOODALL*

You have made it to the final MAKE BIG HAPPEN RHYTHM, lucky number 7! And in case you have not noticed by now, each new rhythm has increased in frequency from the previous rhythm, from multiyear to annual to quarterly to monthly to bimonthly to weekly, and finally to daily.

This final business rhythm focuses on developing skills—skills of the company through hiring and firing as well as your own personal skills:

1. **Focusing on A players**—getting the best people in the right seats and best practices associated with candidate acquisition.

2. **Self-assessment**—knowing how you and your teammates behave under pressure and what motivates the behavior can be game-changing for you and your teams.

3. **Candid, constructive feedback**—giving your people the opportunity to learn and improve by sharing feedback with them on their strengths and weaknesses.

4. **Time management**—never seem to have enough time to get done what you really need to? We will show you how through several time management techniques.

5. **Continuous learning**—top performers are always learning.

While you will likely not perform every practice every day, these practices must occupy a reasonable mindshare.

Focusing on A Players

After coaching hundreds of top-achieving CEOs, we can tell you that the number one difference between top companies and everyone else is the quality of leaders on the team. Winning CEOs surround themselves with other winners. They stack their C-suites with A performers—no excuses and no compromises. They do not hold on to B and C performers because they do not want to turn into Bs or Cs themselves. They know all the reasons that bad CEOs stick with middling performers, and they know that all those reasons are junk:

- A well-liked nice guy who's slipping? Sorry, nice guy is not a job.

- A solid B performer? B performers lead to B companies that get eaten alive in adversity.

- Worried you might be firing an underperformer who could improve? Don't. The bigger—and more common risk—is keeping a weak performer who never improves.

- Cannot afford to hire the best person for the job? Crunch the numbers. What would an A talent add to your bottom line? Most likely, you cannot afford *not* to hire that person.

- A longtime colleague who has been with the company since the beginning? The people who got you where you are today often cannot take you where you want to go next.

- Afraid of rocking the boat and upsetting the staff? You are the CEO! If you will not make tough calls that push the company forward, who will?

To paraphrase Jim Collins's excellent book *Good to Great*, people are not your company's most important asset. The *right* people are the people who, like you, are not going to settle for good enough day in and day out, who will do great work, and who push the rest of your staff to do the same.

Do not saddle your A performers with mediocrities; go out and get more As. And do not let sentiment—or worse, fear—come between you and the staff your company deserves. To meaningfully outperform the competition, you must have the best A players on your team, period.

Top companies fill their firms with top performers. Why? Because in business, as Steve Jobs put it, "A small team of A+ players can run circles around a giant team of B and C players." Stop for a second and let that quote from Jobs sink in.

Now, ask yourself, "How many B and C players fill the top 20 percent of the highest-paid people in my company?"

To that same audience of six hundred CEOs and entrepreneurs Mark recently asked whether they know what success in their business looks like, he also posed the question "How many of you would honestly rate every member of your leadership team as an A performer?" Not a single hand went up. He asks that question every time he speaks, and the answer is usually the same.

Most companies are stocked with average performers because it is the path of least resistance. What you end up with is people who perform just enough to not get fired but not great enough to generate rocket ship growth.

To be a high-growth company, you must continually raise the bar of performance expectation. Yesterday's A performers could be tomorrow's B or C performers if you are not careful. Often, you will find that the people who got you to where you are today are not the same people who will get you to where you want to go tomorrow. Not everybody can or wants to grow as fast as you do.

McKinsey published a study based on six hundred thousand individuals that showed top performers in highly complex occupations were on average eight times more productive than average performers. Think about that. Eight times! What would be the impact on your business if you added more of these high-impact players and fewer (or none) of these average performers? This is why you cannot settle for anyone but top players if you want to build a meaningful company.[7]

Look, we know it is no fun to fire underperformers who are good people whom you have been working with for many years, who have a family that you have shared great moments with. Yet, we have never met a CEO who said, "I fired them too soon." They all told us they felt a lot worse when they realized they waited too long to make a necessary change that would have occurred anyway. The longest time in a leader's life is the time between the moment that they lose confidence in someone and the moment they do something about it.

> When our longtime client Rich Balot was in his twenties, things were not going well on the home front. His father had been unemployed for a few years, and his mom was about to divorce him. Rich looked around and saw that cell phones were taking off, so he thought it would be a great idea to start a cell phone business. To get started, he partnered with his brother, hired their dad, opened the first store, and started riding the cell phone wave.

---

7   Scott Keller and Mary Meaney, "Attracting and retaining the right talent," McKinsey. com, November 24, 2017, https://www.mckinsey.com/business-functions/ organization/our-insights/attracting-and-retaining-the-right-talent.

The company grew rapidly until at one point it was over-expanded, and the finances had clearly become a mess. Rich hired a CFO to try to straighten things out. Rich described the less-than-rigorous qualifications he used when hiring: "He's been a CFO. I like him. He knows the accounting side, so I hired him." Not surprisingly, things went south quickly.

The CFO came from a manufacturing background but did not know small-box retail accounting and the importance of having individual store P&Ls. As a result, he was not able to give Rich the information he needed to make the tough decisions to turn the business around. Compounding his problem, Rich said, "I decided that he was the wrong person probably three to four months before I finally got rid of him. I'll bet you I aged more in those three to four months than any other time in my life."

And the management turnover did not stop there.

At this point, Rich hired Mark Moses as his coach, and we realized his head of sales had to go too. The only problem was that this guy was a close, personal friend of Rich's. So, we moved him to another role where he would be a better fit and replaced him with one of the best sales leaders in the business.

We continued to upgrade Rich's staff year after year to ensure we had the absolute best people in each role. And it paid off. In 2015, Rich merged his company with a much bigger one, retained a 20 percent interest in it, and became the chairman and co-CEO of a $750 million juggernaut.

But that is not the end of the story.

About a year after the merger, we hired a senior executive from a publicly traded company to become the new CEO. This new guy was not a big believer in coaching—was too busy for that—so our gig was up. Over the next two years, the company grew fast, but the culture got messed up. What used to be a sales organization became a cost-cutting organization, and it was super unhealthy.

Turnover within the stores—salespeople, the store managers—had gone to historically high levels, and it was having an extremely negative impact on the culture. Sales was blaming ops. Ops did not like sales. It was becoming toxic.

By early 2019, the CEO had resigned, and Rich stepped back in as the head guy. The company now had $1.7 billion in annual revenue, more than one thousand stores, and nearly six thousand employees. Rich brought Mark back in to coach him and the team.

We restarted the annual, quarterly, and weekly planning rhythm—the MAKE BIG HAPPEN SYSTEM. We hired a rock star sales leader from a competitor to lead the sales team and replaced three out of four regional vice presidents who'd reported to the old guy. Then we went down a level and replaced sixteen out of twenty-four of the district managers with new all-stars. We kept digging down to each level and replacing the bad actors with people who can take the company to its next leg of BIG growth.

In short order, just by changing a few key players and putting the MAKE BIG HAPPEN SYSTEM back in place, company sales and profitability rose meaningfully, and the culture has improved dramatically. With Rich's commitment to the MAKE BIG HAPPEN SYSTEM, he went from near bankruptcy to the creation of a one-thousand-plus-location retail empire, producing a *nine-figure* cash event for himself and setting his company up for sustained year-over-year growth. When the new organization went off track, Rich's decision to recommit the company to the MAKE BIG HAPPEN SYSTEM turned it around and produced an even bigger outcome, growing to nearly $2 billion in sales and continuing its record of strong growth to this day.

Rich Balot and his team after Rich took back control as CEO

Hiring the right people with the right skills and firing the wrong fits are both necessary and difficult. You need courage, support, and a structured process to make your decisions. We will share two types of tools that will help you (1) select the right talent within a qualified pool of candidates and (2) evaluate the quality of your current leadership team.

Why Having the Best People in Your Company Matters

Having the best people in your company is the most important thing you can do to grow and sustain a fast-growing business. Here are four reasons why you should go above and beyond to get the best people possible for every position:

1. **A company cannot be more successful than the quality of the people who populate it.** Just as a chain will never be stronger than its weakest link, your company will never be stronger than its weakest person. If you want to perform in the top 1 percent of your peer group, you need the absolute best people in every key role.

2. **You will create a virtuous cycle.** Top people want to be around other top people. If you create a reputation for having the best people in the industry, you will be a magnet and draw other top performers.

3. **You will have fewer headaches.** Poor performers create messes and drama. Top performers create results. Which do you want?

4. **You will get to where you want to go faster.** A top-tier performer can get eight times the results of an average performer. Get a few of those top performers on your team, and, well, you can do the math and see where that takes you.

Richard Paek, CEO, and Bob Seidmeyer, COO, of Texas-based Jiffy Lube franchisee Allied Lube, are closely familiar with the power of having top talent in the executive leadership team. The two leaders have locked arms together very effectively to drive operational productivity, and they've filled their C-suite with other top leaders.

In Richard's words, "Having A players like Bob has allowed me to focus on the big picture and allows me to explore options in the future. It's only possible because of the confidence I have in having Bob and his team be able to execute on the things we decide to do. I'm able to look at acquisitions, financing, tax planning, and culture. I'm able to focus on the future, even out further than ten years. I'm able to get key information in real time that I need to be able to be the visionary of Allied. With Bob and his operational team, I feel I'm on top of things without having to spend a great deal of time getting into details of his world. We have our one-on-one calls once a week, which allow us to do our jobs effectively."

Richard's COO, Bob, commented on Richard's leadership, saying, "Having an owner that shares his vision and goals with myself and operations allows us to keep Allied moving forward in a positive direction. Richard follows through on what he says he will do and expects the same from his staff and leadership team. Richard does not micromanage us, which allows and forces us to think on our feet. He is no drama and doesn't sugarcoat, frequently saying, 'Bring me ideas, solutions, and recommendations. Don't blame others—let's admit to our mistakes and let's move on.' Richard's constant thinking and craftiness keep the company motivated and wanting to do more. He's honest, trusts but verifies with his team, challenges us to reach the next level, and is always thinking about the employees. When I wake up, I am still excited to go to work and do the impossible. There are lots of jobs and companies out there, but Allied Lube is my family, and that's because Richard has made it that way."

Allied Lube CEO Richard Paek and his team receive the Franchisee of the Year Award from Jiffy Lube for exemplifying excellence across their eighty service centers.

Selecting and Evaluating New Talent

Here are four ways a better talent-selection process will help ensure you have the absolute best people running your company:

1. **Attracting and selecting the best leaders.** Our formalized process helps ensure you do not get blindsided by somebody who is a good talker but not a great achiever.

2. **Removing the unfit leaders.** Sometimes you must let a

person go to make room for a much more talented leader.

3. **Retaining and motivating the top leaders.** The best want to work with the best, and by creating the right leadership team, you will keep your C-suite motivated and engaged.

4. **Boost profitability.** The right leadership team will get results that drive profits higher.

Our **Candidate Evaluation Checklist** (page 269) will help you identify, select, and onboard the right talent needed for your positions. The right people will:

1. Share your company values

2. Have a proven track record

Successful candidates must check both boxes. When companies fail here, it is because they get folks that excel at one component but not the other. For example, an excellent performer that does not share your values will slowly—or quickly—erode the culture of your company and take other top performers down with them. Do not fall into this trap. If the candidate does not score high in both areas, say "next" and move on.

> **An excellent performer that does not share your values will slowly–or quickly–erode the culture of your company and take other top performers down with them.**

Our **Interview Scoring Matrix** (page 271) does double duty. First, it will be your "scoring matrix" as you interview the candidate, and second, it will be the scoring matrix you use when you talk to the candidate's references. There are two critical areas during the interview process that you want to screen for. You want to be clear on how well the candidate's prior work experience matches up to your company's goals, and you want to discern if the candidate's values line up with your company's values.

You know how much we have emphasized the importance of having the absolute best people on the team. So not surprisingly, this interview process is critically important to the future of your business. Likewise, it is critically important to get intentional about the *employee* value proposition. Most firms get this dialed in for their target clients but not their most important stakeholders: their employees!

Self-Assessment

When you look at yourself in the mirror, what do you see? A study reported in *Harvard Business Review* found that "although 95% of people think they're self-aware, only 10 to 15% actually are."[8] Self-awareness is the ability to see yourself clearly and objectively and to understand how other people see you. It is actually a skill you can develop and a key component of emotional intelligence.

Having a greater degree of self-awareness is critically important and will help you in the following ways:

- Reduce unforced errors in running your business

- Increase your confidence and creativity

- Improve your decision-making

- Enhance your interpersonal relationships and your communication effectiveness

One way we help our clients improve their level of self-awareness is by using a comprehensive third-party TTI Talent Insights assessment, developed by TTI Success Insights, that measures behaviors and driving forces. We recommend TTI Talent Insights assessments to all our clients

---

8   Tasha Eurich, "Working with People Who Aren't Self-Aware," *Harvard Business Review Online* (October 19, 2018), https://hbr.org/2018/10/working-with-people-who-arent-self-aware.

and their teams to help them identify the behavioral patterns and incentives that enable or impede individual and team success.

The tool is based on the almost-century-old Harvard-formulated behavioral sciences known as "DISC." We use the version of DISC from TTI Success Insights. This version, which is augmented by a "crowd-sourced" scientific analysis of over thirty million survey respondents around the world, produces a detailed forty-five-plus-page report with applications that we have been certified to put into practice. With it, you can answer two seemingly simple questions that can have a powerful impact on your company's success:

1. How well does a person's behavioral profile—including my own—align with the actual demands of their specific role at this time?

2. How is someone's behavior or communication—including my own—interpreted by others both naturally and under stress, and how does this affect our ability to function effectively?

TTI Behavioral Insights

The proven science behind DISC classifies our behavior across four separate dimensions:

D: Dominance—how we respond to problems and challenges

I: Influence—how we relate to people and contacts

S: Steadiness—how we respond to changes in pace and consistency

C: Compliance—how we relate to procedures and complaints

Each of these dimensions is scored based on our responses to a scientifically formulated survey. There is no "good" or "bad" mix of these dimensions—just strengths, opportunities, and, yes, blind spots.

Someone who scores on one end of the D scale might be described as ambitious and is probably often viewed as a problem solver. To others on the opposite end of the D spectrum, that same person might sometimes be interpreted as overly aggressive, demanding, and even prone to taking unnecessary risks. A person on one end of the C spectrum would often be seen as organized, data driven, and concerned about accuracy. To their opposites, these same qualities might be interpreted as overly cautious, rigid, and even stubborn.

Job Fit

The most immediate application of these profiles is job fit. We can readily see that some profiles (e.g., such as those that are fast paced) are more naturally aligned with sales roles: opening doors, sometimes getting them slammed in your face, but nonetheless staying the course until you have closed the sale. Other positions require a steadier hand capable of accurately performing repetitive activities and carefully considering quantifiable data. For example, slower-paced and task-oriented profiles tend to be good fits for many finance and engineering positions. It is important to note that there is no inherent value judgment in faster or slower paced—some roles and circumstances call for more of one versus the other. When tasking someone to clear a minefield, you would certainly choose the slower-paced, task-focused individual.

Maybe you have a head of sales whose reliance on slow-paced, people-oriented behaviors and "relationship-sales" style once served you well. But now, maybe what you need to spur rapid growth is a fast-paced and task-oriented or fast-paced and people-oriented person, someone whom Matt Dixon would call a "challenger-sale" style. Is your current head of sales able to make and manage that transformation, or are you setting yourselves up for disappointment and failure by assigning tasks to someone who is not wired to lead them effectively?

To be clear, you would not use a TTI report alone to terminate a head of sales, or anyone for that matter, simply for having the wrong profile. However, you would want to know the profile of your head of sales before embarking on a growth plan. "What might get in your way" in this case would be a head of sales whose behaviors do not adapt well to the new, uncertain road ahead. If your head of sales is a top performer, you might instead get her a coach to guide her through the journey and learn tools and practices to adapt to this new reality. Or you might conclude that she needs a deputy who can drive the correct behaviors. However, defining a sales strategy that requires conductor or persuader behaviors but relies on the experience of a promoter or supporter is not a recipe for success.

You could apply a similar example to any other critical role in your business. For example, do you need a precise, systematic leader in the CFO seat (slower paced and task oriented) but have someone who is fast paced and people oriented—and therefore always looking to be "part of the action"? Among the top two mistakes we have seen companies make are (1) placing a sales profile in finance and (2) placing a financial profile in sales.

Likewise, the same profile might reveal that *you* are not a perfect profile fit for the specific demands of the goals that you have set for yourself. Or that you have surrounded yourself almost exclusively with people who have similar behaviors to yours, creating somewhat of an echo chamber. By contrast, you may have created unnecessary tension by surrounding yourself with people who all react differently to stimulus and incentives. Regardless, you should ask yourself, "Where are the gaps? Do I need someone at my right hand who is more structured to protect me from unnecessary risks? Someone bolder about acting while I rally the troops back at the office? Someone more attuned to the zeitgeist of the leadership team while I charge forth?"

Jim Collins advised us against having the wrong people on the bus. Taking this one step further, do not have the wrong person for the wrong role or for the wrong specific challenge.

Communication

The other key insight from the TTI tool pertains to how we process and communicate information. For example, fast-moving, task-oriented profiles tend to make decisions very quickly and assume that everyone sees the same "picture" of the destination in their heads. They have seen this movie before and know how it ends. But do the slower-paced leaders on your team see the same ending? Do they see any ending at all? If you are the faster-paced person, have you adequately articulated the roadmap for where you are going so your key people can follow you and point out the occasional speed bump along the way? In any of these cases, "what might get in your way" are competing interpretations of the plan or costly drama and tension among your leadership team due to poor communication.

Along the lines of drama, do you have several high-dominance, high-influence people on your leadership team? They probably spend lots of time fighting for the microphone, so to speak, talking over one another in meetings and pulling you into competitions for influence. You neutralize this by using the TTI report to shed light on these traits, encouraging your leaders to make personal commitments based on better self-awareness, and instituting some simple rules of engagement that clearly define each leader's more autonomous and shared spheres of authority.

The age-old stereotypical tension between engineering and sales can often be reduced to differing TTI profiles as well. The engineers, often coordinators, view sales as too eager to make costly promises that the company cannot keep and too eager to charge forward with exciting new products. The salespeople, often persuaders, see the engineering team as too cautious, too slow, and too structured to give them the tools they need to hit their goals. The TTI reports offer specific, customized guidance to help each party communicate with the other and a common language that coordinators can use to get through to persuaders when it really matters, and vice versa.

At the same time, your people deserve to understand how best to communicate with you. If you are a task-oriented person, it might behoove you to ask your head of sales to slow down, stop "selling you," and offer details and evidence to back up her requests. Their natural inclination will be to convince you with words, not data. By contrast, if you are fast paced, you need to know that the trains will be arriving on time but not be bothered by how the schedule is built. Either way, your team deserves to know how to give you the information that you need in a way that you are likely to hear.

Here is a specific example. Chris Larkins is a mix of persuader and conductor, very fast paced and an even mix of task oriented and people oriented. Prior to joining CEO Coaching International, one of his operations leaders (let's call him Ed) was a coordinator, also task oriented but considerably slower paced. He was an excellent employee and a perfect profile fit for the demands of his specific job. Nonetheless, when Ed would knock on his door each morning, Chris came to feel a slight sense of unease. To Chris, these morning updates seemed to involve Ed taking ten minutes to tell Chris that "he had no news." Chris found himself avoiding what might be important information. Worse, his frustration was likely being observed by Ed.

Ed, being a coordinator, simply wanted Chris to understand that while he might not have an answer for a question that Chris asked yesterday, he did everything reasonable to try to get one. Ed's TTI profile values accuracy and thoroughness, which he would put on display by starting his morning updates by describing all the things he did to try to get an answer. To Ed, this was simply reasonable diligence. To Chris, it was "taking ten minutes to tell me you have no news."

Reflecting on the situation and realizing that Ed was a coordinator, Chris called him into his office. To defuse the tension, Chris offered Ed some advice based entirely on insights from each of their TTI reports. "When you knock on my door in the morning to give me an update," Chris said, "start with the headline." This instantly gave Chris options in response to Ed's "headline": "Sit down and tell me more" or "Interesting, but I'm tied up this morning. Can you come back after lunch and tell me more?" or "Don't worry, I didn't expect you to have an answer so soon. Come back when you do." Similarly, Chris learned to share expectations more clearly with Ed—not every question required an answer within a day or even a week, and Chris was careful to distinguish for Ed those things that were urgent and those that would reasonably take more time to resolve.

The experience led Chris to repeat the exercise with his entire leadership team, each from the perspective of their own unique TTI profiles.

Tera Peterson, cofounder of cosmetics industry leader NuFACE, recently hired a new CEO for the company so she can take a step back from the day-to-day responsibilities of the business to instead serve as chairman of the board. TTI profiles were not only instrumental in helping her select the right candidate for that role, but she also uses them regularly with her team to enhance productivity in their business.

"They're spot on. An amazing tool, especially when you have a coach to guide you through it," Tera says. "It's so helpful for knowing how to communicate to your colleagues in a way they'll be receptive to. By having a common language through the report, you don't take challenges in collaboration as personally."

NuFACE's new rock star CEO has not only over twenty years of experience growing companies in the cosmetics industry, but he also has the personal behaviors and motivations that will lead to the greatest productivity in the management suite. "Tera and her team are on track to deliver EBITDA in 2021 five times greater than in 2019," reports her coach Alberto Carvalho.

Driving Forces

There is a second aspect to the TTI Success Insights tool that helps us to understand the "driving forces" behind *why* we behave the way we do.

A driving force is what makes a person get out of bed, excited for the day. It is why we do what we do. When your driving forces are satisfied, you feel engaged, rewarded, and energized. People who are passionate about what they are doing perform at a much higher level.

Backed by thirty years of research, TTI Success Insights identifies twelve driving forces that represent the ends of a spectrum across six motivators.

INSTINCTIVE	THEORETICAL	INTELLECTUAL
People who are driven by utilizing past experiences, intuition and seeking specific knowledge when necessary.	KNOWLEDGE	People who are driven by opportunities to learn, acquire knowledge and the discovery of truth.
SELFLESS	UTILITARIAN	RESOURCEFUL
People who are driven by completing tasks for the greater good, with little expectation of personal return.	UTILITY	People who are driven by practical results, maximizing both efficiency and returns for their investments of time, talent, energy and resources.
OBJECTIVE	AESTHETIC	HARMONIOUS
People who are driven by the functionality and objectivity of their surroundings.	SURROUNDINGS	People who are driven by the experience, subjective viewpoints and balance in their surroundings.
INTENTIONAL	SOCIAL	ALTRUISTIC
People who are driven to assist others for a specific purpose, not just for the sake of being helpful or supportive.	OTHERS	People who are driven by the benefits they provide others.
COLLABORATIVE	INDIVIDUALISTIC	COMMANDING
People who are driven by being in a supporting role and contributing with little need for individual recognition.	POWER	People who are driven by status, recognition and control over personal freedom.
RECEPTIVE	TRADITIONAL	STRUCTURED
People who are driven by new ideas, methods and opportunities that fall outside a defined system for living.	METHODOLOGIES	People who are driven by traditional approaches, proven methods and a defined system for living.

Copyright Target Training International Ltd.

Driving forces exist in everyone, from the CEO to the receptionist. The more the forces are satisfied, the more engaged your team members will be. We tend to see the world through the window of our top three to four driving forces, called our primary cluster.

What drives one team can be quite different from what drives another team. Think about the differences in what motivates your sales team versus your finance team, as an example. While there are clear differences, there is nothing wrong about them. There is no "right" answer.

The TTI driving forces tool can therefore offer personal guidance to you and your leadership team about how to structure your environment, processes, and/or incentives to encourage more of the behaviors that fit the demands of your strategy or the moment.

At the same time, the driving forces component of the Talent Insights profile can offer personalized insights as to what might cause someone's behavior to diverge from their natural DISC behavioral profile—for example, why your fast-paced, people-oriented salesperson might suddenly be acting as anything but that. Simply put, the current environment might not be motivating them to embody their natural behavior, causing a shift under stress. This is an invaluable tool for sitting with this person, diagnosing what might be causing that stress, and developing a plan to neutralize it.

Reviewing everyone's Talent Insights profile—and the strengths, opportunities, blind spots, and strategies for effective communication—is so valuable to helping a team work more effectively together that it is a best practice to incorporate this into your annual planning process.

Avoid Sabotage

The TTI Talent Insights assessment is an indispensable element to help you avoid some of the most common things that might get in your way—the often silent and overlooked factors that can sabotage the best-laid plans. This tool will help you to do the following:

1. Understand how you are naturally driven to respond in different circumstances and how this might cause you to get in your own way. Using these insights to build a more balanced team, one whose behaviors complement your own in the pursuit of your goals, can help you fill gaps on your team, and improve your chances of success.

2. Appreciate how the profiles of your leadership team align with the behaviors that your vision and goals require at this moment in time. You must have the right person in the right seat for the right task—someone armed with natural behaviors to leverage the opportunities and overcome the challenges that accompany your plan.

3. Learn how you should communicate with your team, how they should communicate with you, and how they should communicate with one another. Better alignment of expectations and a reduction in tension is a natural result.

4. Discover how to motivate certain behaviors over others, depending on the demands of the moment. The ability to offer personalized guidance to your leadership team and identify opportunities to neutralize pressure will allow your team to be more productive.

Once you complete this TTI Talent Insights assessment and get debriefed by a certified professional, you will discover new things about your behavior and your motivators. With this new insight, you will be more "self-aware" of the behaviors and motivators that are working for you and the ones that are working against you. Likewise, you will be able to see these in others and become more effective in how you deal with them.

One other tip here: complete this assessment for your entire leadership team and then do a debrief for everybody. You will learn all kinds of new things about your colleagues and discover more effective ways of working together.

Hopefully, we have convinced you of the power of the TTI Talent Insights assessment and it takes its place in your arsenal of tools as a leader. However, it is important that you rely on someone who is trained and certified to interpret the profiles. Our brief introduction above does not by any means make you an expert or qualified to interpret the results on your own.

Candid, Constructive Feedback

Top performers recognize that everyone has strengths and weaknesses, skills, and blind spots. They are committed to continuous improvement and open minded to constructive feedback from those around them. Brutally honest feedback can sting sometimes, but it is important to know that if appreciated, absorbed, and implemented, it can be a powerful force in helping you grow into being a better leader. Our **Leadership Team 360° Review** (page 273) lists the right questions for team members to be asking one another to discover where to devote energy to improve their leadership and management behaviors.

The feedback will be most valuable if collected anonymously, as the removal of the fear of how the commentary will be perceived will cause those giving it to be more candid and direct. Using a coach who is not involved in the day-to-day operations of the business is helpful for this exercise so that team members' input can be collected and presented by an unbiased party.

Time Management

Business success is not simply a line sloping upward to the right. Instead, it is filled with squiggles, setbacks, and near-death moments that can shake the very foundation of your business. And certainly, some of these confidence-draining moments are unavoidable and likely due to factors outside your control. But many others are self-inflicted wounds that are predictable and preventable.

Effective leaders anticipate what could get in the way, and they solve the problem before it ever gets big enough to become one.

> These high-impact activities are the ones you tend to postpone, waiting for a time in which you are free from daily problems. Unfortunately, you will be dead before that free time arrives.

As a CEO, you know your time is extremely valuable, but it is still easy to let the urgent distract you from the important. If something has an immediate deadline, we tend to prioritize it, because we want to get it off our plate. And as a CEO, we know this pressure to focus your attention on the immediate matters that pop up each day will never set you free from the tyranny of the whirlwind.

It has been our experience that there is often an inverse correlation between what is "urgent" and what's "important" as it relates to the long-term success of your company. The mismatch occurs because issues with immediate deadlines are often the ones that contribute less to the long-term success of your company, while the strategic and relevant matters that impact the profitability and the sustainability of your business the most are the ones without an immediate deadline. These high-impact activities are the ones you tend to postpone, waiting for a time in which you are free from daily problems. Unfortunately, you will be dead before that free time arrives.

CEO Coaching International coach Bill Whitehead counsels his clients to get back to the basics of time blocking. And in particular, he recommends scheduling a "power hour" each day where you make it clear to everybody that you do not want to be distracted unless the building is on fire. And in this block, you take time to think deeply about the business, to scan the horizon and anticipate issues that might arise. With clear thinking time, you intentionally take a break from the daily rush and reset your focus on the bigger picture.

Georgetown professor Cal Newport takes the power hour idea to an extreme and recommends what he calls "deep work." In simple terms, it is about spending several hours, days, or weeks at a time engrossed in "deep" rather than "shallow" work. The key is to have long stretches of uninterrupted time to focus on your highest-value activities.

Bill Gates is famous for (among other things) his seven-day "think weeks" that he took twice a year during his time running Microsoft. Cut off from civilization, he spent up to eighteen hours a day in a remote cabin in the Pacific Northwest devouring books and articles and pondering the future.

If you had an extra hour every day, what would you work on? When we ask this question, most CEOs answer by saying they would focus on the bigger picture, longer-term factors that would most impact the company such as the strategy, improving sales processes, and reducing operating costs. But the funny thing is, during their normal workday, they spend little time on these critical areas.

Why?

CEOs, as do most busy human beings, tend to focus first on the issues that are urgent and second—sometimes a distant second—on the issues that are important. We flip that reality using our **Power Hour Planner** tool (page 275). It will help you focus on what really matters and what will move the needle in your company. Its strength lies in its simplicity. It asks you to methodically freeze one hour per day in which you isolate yourself from any distraction and focus your attention on the high-priority activities of the quarter.

David Sobel worked for thirteen years at Home Warranty of America. He built a replicable and scalable sales model that massively accelerated sales and led to a $50 million sale of the company. Now he is a coach here at CEO Coaching International.

How did he drive the company's sales growth?

He understood how long-term goals must be broken down into clear, shorter-term goals that can inspire people and motivate them to succeed. If you think small, you will remain small, but BIG goals lead to exponential improvement. Why? It is a shift in mindset and action. If you start thinking BIG, you will start acting BIG. If you clearly understand what you need to achieve in one year, you can break it down to what you need to do in a month, a week, and a day. As David says, "You win the year by winning the day."

Another suggestion to help you effectively manage your time is the concept of the ten-minute unscheduled call. This is an amazingly simple principle that can reduce time slippage. No unscheduled meeting or phone call should last more than ten minutes. Whenever someone calls you without having scheduled the call, let them know you have a hard stop in ten minutes. Then offer them a choice: they can either schedule a call with you when you have more time to address the issue, or they can take up to ten minutes now and get it resolved. Most of the time, they will take the ten minutes now. This is a win-win because it reduces time wasted on your and the caller's side. This also leads to better results, because it forces the person you are conversing with to be clear and concise. This is a simple hack that saves time and improves effectiveness.

Another small change that can have a big impact is to tell your team to minimize carbon copying emails and only copy you via BCC, so that when others reply to all, you will not receive all replies. All too often CEOs get trapped in a chain of emails that take your focus off the big items. Create a culture of efficiency, and everyone will respect not only your time but one another's time.

Continuous Learning

You do not need us to tell you the business world is spinning faster these days. And if you do not start learning faster than the world is changing, you will get dumber by the day. Our **Continuous Learning Tracking Sheet** (page 277) helps you organize the key areas where you need to focus your learning and map out a game plan to be a top student. Few things are more important to your success as a leader than being a lifelong learner.

It has almost become cliché to talk about disruption, exponential technology, artificial intelligence, and robots. However, there is a reason we read and hear about these topics all the time. Disruption is real, and companies that are slow to adapt to the pace of change will get rolled over. Learning—and acting on what you learn—is the key to staying relevant.

Nolan Bushnell, the founder of Atari and numerous other companies, is a consummate continuous learner. On a podcast with Michael Gervais, Bushnell said he likes to travel "low budget," visiting different countries and immersing himself in the culture, since you do not really learn much staying at a Four Seasons. For business ideas, he attends random trade shows and walks the exhibit hall just to learn new things and pick up ideas. Creativity kicks in by connecting the dots of what he has learned from these disparate inputs. The key is to have a large number of dots that you can connect to one another.

Your competitors are always looking for ways to put you out of business. Just like the employee who got you where you are today might not be the same as who gets you to the next step, the products and services that built your company may not be the ones to carry you into the future. Your competitors, who might be in a garage or in China, Vietnam, or Palo Alto right now, are ready to pounce and chip away at your market position.

Like Bushnell, have an unquenchable thirst for learning, and make it part of your company's culture. If there is a bubbling trend in your industry, explore it. If you are seeing unexpected things in the industry, follow your curiosity. We are not suggesting you go chasing white rabbits down a hole. However, be curious and inquisitive.

Summary: MAKE BIG HAPPEN
RHYTHM 7—Increase Productivity

Developing your skills and the skills of your employees to increase productivity throughout your company requires daily attention.

RHYTHM FREQUENCY	DAILY

TOOL	REFERENCE
Candidate Evaluation Checklist	Page 269
Interview Scoring Matrix	Page 271
Leadership Team 360° Review	Page 273
Power Hour Planner	Page 275
Continuous Learning Tracking Sheet	Page 277

Throughout this chapter we provided clear and concise overviews of how to hold the different meetings that give structure to the MAKE BIG HAPPEN RHYTHMS and challenge you to build a stronger company.

Here is a reminder of the meeting cadence that serves as the foundation to the MAKE BIG HAPPEN RHYTHMS:

OPTIMIZED MEETINGS

ANNUALLY | Rhythm 2	Annual Planning Session Annual Company All-Hands
QUARTERLY | Rhythm 3	Quarterly Alignment Session Quarterly Company All-Hands
MONTHLY | Rhythm 4	Financial Performance Review Monthly Strategic Review
BI-MONTHLY | Rhythm 5	Bi-Monthly Accountability Session
WEEKLY | Rhythm 6	Move-the-Needle Session Weekly Leadership Meeting Weekly Departmental Team Meeting One-on-Ones

Apply the MAKE BIG HAPPEN QUESTIONS to Take Action

MAKE BIG HAPPEN SYSTEM: Element 2—Applying the MAKE BIG HAPPEN QUESTIONS

The wise man doesn't give the right answers,
he poses the right questions.
—*CLAUDE LEVI-STRAUSS*

Sarah Dusek and her husband, Jacob, founders of glamping business Under Canvas, had just opened for their first season on ten acres of land six miles outside of Yellowstone National Park. The camp was filled with eager glampers clamoring for a slice of Mother Nature, and Sarah was ecstatic that the business was up and running after immeasurable hard work.

Suddenly, ominous clouds rolled in. Before long, wind, rain, lightning, and thunder came whipping through and flattened everything Sarah had built. As she watched in horror, she thought, "This is crazy. It's over. There is no more Under Canvas for us."

With only two choices—give up or move forward—she chose to rise to the challenge.

In 2018 Sarah attended our CEO Coaching International Summit, an annual gathering of top entrepreneurs and CEOs from around the world, where we gave every attendee a glass plaque with the words "What do you want?" etched on it.

"I looked at that thing for three days, and I actually started to ask myself that question. We'd now been in business almost ten years, and I started to ask, where are we going? What is our trajectory? Yes, I'm building this company to grow it, but what is it I really want? What does success look like for my company? What does it look like for me, personally?" said Sarah.

Sarah and Jacob set goals that were just out of reach for the resources Under Canvas had. Setting goals that stretch the limits of what's possible forces leaders to use constraints as a source of creative innovation. And from that shaky beginning, Sarah's company began to grow.

Working with her coach at CEO Coaching International, she decided what outcome she wanted to achieve through RHYTHM 1, set an annual growth target through RHYTHM 2, and then broke it down into the initiatives, activities, and KPIs they would have to achieve to make that goal a reality and executed with discipline through the rest of the rhythms.

Within a year, Sarah and Jake sold their company for a nine-figure sum at a 32x multiple of EBITDA. That is the power of a vision underpinned by strong values and clear goals. That is the power of not taking no for an answer. That is the power of knowing the answer to the question "What do you want?"

Under Canvas CEO Sarah Dusek knows the sky's the limit for the future of her company.

In *MAKE BIG HAPPEN*, we introduced four critical questions every business leader should explore on their journey to business and life success. The four questions, called the MAKE BIG HAPPEN QUESTIONS, are as follows:

1. What do you want? (**Vision**)

2. What do you have to do? (**Action**)

3. What could get in the way? (**Anticipate**)

4. How do you hold yourself accountable? (**Measure**)

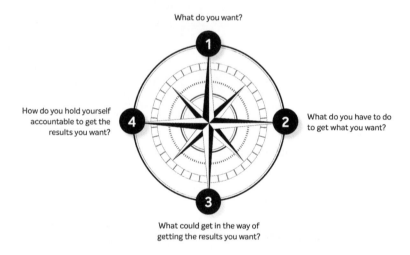

By answering these four questions, you create the foundation for a fast-growing, profitable business. The questions are universal, but the power in this framework is in your ability to apply it to all types of challenges, from strategic to tactical, and all levels of your organization, from the C-suite to the frontline workforce.

APPLYING THE MAKE BIG HAPPEN QUESTIONS TO COMMON CHALLENGES

Applying the MAKE BIG HAPPEN QUESTIONS is an iterative process, where each question builds on itself. Let's look at applying the framework to a strategic example we often find the C-suite struggling to answer:

Example 1: Setting Annual Goals

1. What do you want?

    Using our MAKE BIG HAPPEN **Crystal Ball** tool in an annual planning session, we challenge the leadership team to define their *lagging* indicators of success that they want to achieve by the end of the year in the form of specific and measurable outcomes.

2. What do you have to do?

    Our MAKE BIG HAPPEN **Crystal Ball** tool challenges the team to define one to three specific and measurable *leading* indicators that will drive each outcome we want from question 1. These leading indicators are then translated into force-ranked initiatives that will drive us to do the things we have to do to achieve what we want.

3. What could get in the way?

    Our MAKE BIG HAPPEN **Initiative Charter** tool challenges the team to think through the many risks that could get in the way of our success, along with a mitigation plan for each risk.

4. How do you hold yourself accountable?

Our MAKE BIG HAPPEN **Company Scorecard** helps you design a game that the team can win by keeping score of the outcomes (what you want), tracking the initiatives that drive the outcomes (what you have to do), and continuously assessing the risks (what could get in the way).

Gaining alignment on a specific and focused set of annual goals is one of the best practices that top-growing firms employ to maintain healthy growth.

Yet not all problems are cross-functional. Often, a client will encounter a tactical problem within a department. Applying the MAKE BIG HAPPEN QUESTIONS solves these types of problems equally as well.

Example 2: Solve Sales Conversion Issues

1. What do you want?

   One of the most frequently asked questions by business leaders is "How do I increase sales?" The VP of sales or similar role is often tasked with solving this challenge. The first step is to unpack what you genuinely want in the form of specific and measurable outcomes. Of course, we often want more than one thing, which requires prioritization to focus effort on the most important outcomes. For example, in answer to "What do you want?" you cannot stop at "Increase sales." Keep asking the question as you dig deeper and deeper:

   Increase sales:

   - Increase sales

     - From new customers or existing?

- From higher unit price or from more units per customer?

  - From existing products/services or new?

Each level of the question hierarchy above can result in vastly different outcomes, and hence vastly different activities to drive the outcomes.

2. What do you have to do?

   Let's assume question 1 resulted in an increased quantity of new customers for our existing product line from 100 per month to 125 per month (i.e., a 25 percent increase in sales quantity). Then ask yourself, "What do I have to do to achieve this outcome?" Using our **Leading-Lagging Indicator Sequence** tool, you identify the conversion rate of existing pipeline leads as the top leading indicator to drive an increase in sales. To drive improvements in conversion rate, our sales managers commit to at least four hours of role-playing per week per salesperson to practice the common objections at each stage of the sales pipeline. The sales management is betting that an increase in role-playing will drive an increase in conversion rate, which will in turn drive an increase in sales from new customers.

3. What could get in the way?

   One of the most obvious risks to our sales improvement plan is the ability of our sales team to make the time to role-play. Most salespeople do not want to take time away to train or practice because they believe they should be spending more time selling. Another is the ability to develop quality role-playing scenarios that move the needle on our conversion rates. By identifying the risks up front, we can then empower the team to overcome the risks before they are realized. There are only so many objections, and most salespeople are not particularly good at handling the main objections. Sometimes, their sales manager or even the president of the company is needed to help close deals, but the salesperson's ego gets in the way and they will not ask for help.

4. How do you hold yourself accountable?

    Using our **Goal Scoreboard** tool, the sales leadership would document the baseline conversion metrics, along with actual role-playing time per salesperson per week. The bet is that the investment in role-playing will move the conversion needle in a positive direction. By measuring the leading indicator (i.e., hours of role-playing per salesperson per week) against the outcome (e.g., conversion rate at each stage of the sales funnel), we can hold the team accountable to achieving what we want.

You will encounter countless tactical challenges on your path to growth. Knowing how to apply the MAKE BIG HAPPEN QUESTIONS under any situation is critical to maintaining your growth year after year.

> **As your company experiences continued growth, it often outgrows the skills of leaders within the team.**

As your company experiences continued growth, it often outgrows the skills of leaders within the team. To ensure you are not one of those leaders, apply the MAKE BIG HAPPEN QUESTIONS to yourself.

Example 3: Develop My Leadership Skills

1. What do you want?

   By using the TTI Talent Insights assessment, you identified a challenge with your communication style that you would like to improve. Specifically, you have a high dominance factor that causes you to immediately overreact with anger when you are confronted with a situation you do not like. You have noticed that this is killing the morale of your leadership team.

2. What do you have to do?

   Your first step is in recognizing there is a problem, followed by having a strong desire to change. Next, you work with your coach to serve as an accountability partner and to practice techniques to overcome your instinct to get angry. You also inform your leadership team that you recognize you have a communications challenge and are actively trying to improve. By humbling yourself and asking your team for help, you have taken a huge first step to fixing the morale problem.

3. What could get in the way?

   You are only human. Fixing ingrained behaviors will not happen overnight. Be prepared for setbacks and be sure to review them with your coach so she can identify the teachable moments and suggest next steps.

4. How do you hold yourself accountable?

   By publicly admitting the problem and the desire to change, you are enlisting others to help hold you accountable to changing your behavior. Using a journal, document the times you failed to keep your anger in check and review the data with your coach to identify any triggers that might help you develop appropriate strategies.

As you can see in the simple examples above, success is achieved by applying the MAKE BIG HAPPEN QUESTIONS in an iterative fashion, along with the help of our MAKE BIG HAPPEN TOOLS, to solve any challenge that gets in the way of growing your business and at any level of the organization.

USING THE MAKE BIG HAPPEN QUESTIONS TO ACHIEVE MASSIVE GROWTH

Since the time of publishing *MAKE BIG HAPPEN*, numerous clients have achieved extraordinary growth by answering our MAKE BIG HAPPEN QUESTIONS.

When we met Brad Caton, he was simultaneously running a janitorial business, landscaping business, and snow-removal business in Vancouver, British Columbia, Canada. He thought that because the businesses were seasonal, it was necessary to run all three.

However, being pulled in so many different directions was driving him crazy.

We asked him MAKE BIG HAPPEN QUESTION 1. "What do you want, Brad?"

His response was understandable: "I want to be a successful businessman and have more time for my family."

After taking a close look at the companies' financials, we found that the margins of two of the businesses were very slim, whereas the other had much greater potential. We recommended he do something that sounded crazy at first: sell the janitorial business, sell the landscaping business, and run the winter snow-removal business full time.

Because of the strategic change, Brad was able to fully focus in on the specific and measurable activities to keep score on to achieve the outcomes he wanted. He implemented the MAKE BIG HAPPEN RHYTHMS, and his coach held him accountable to the key metrics that mattered most.

Today Brad's company, Invictus Professional Snow-fighters, provides snow-removal and ice-management services 365 days a year. Since implementing the MAKE BIG HAPPEN SYSTEM, Brad has tripled the size of the business, and profits are up over 400 percent. And in the summer, when it is not snowing, Brad certainly has more time to spend with his family.

Every successful leader reaches a point where the grind feels exhausting, the results seem underwhelming, and you start to question whether you are making a difference. Maybe you just lost your best client, or maybe you have been working seventy hours a week with no end in sight and feel no closer to your destination. Perhaps you are just questioning if you have really got what it takes to achieve your goals.

Ron Carson, founder of the financial advisory firm Carson Group, had one of those days back at the beginning of his career in Omaha, Nebraska. Ron was in his car, driving back to his office after being stood up on a key appointment, upon which he had been staking high hopes. He had not gained a single client all month.

At the time, he was just a few years into the business and had little to show for it. As Ron drove, he told himself, "I have to do something different, or this is it."

Not knowing where to start and simply wanting to hear a friendly voice on the other end of the line, Ron returned to his office and began to call his top clients, out of the blue and without an agenda. To his surprise, his clients were shocked that he called for no reason: no new product to pitch them, no action required on their portfolio, just checking in to say hello. During a time when the financial services industry was overwhelmingly transactional, clients did not know how to respond to a simple "Hi, how are you doing?"

This is when Ron first realized that he could build a business on the foundation of putting clients first. He asked himself a simple question, "What do I have to do?" and realized the answer was to make his clients such raving fans that the company would grow like wildfire from word-of-mouth referrals.

In time, Carson Group's private wealth business grew to approximately $1 billion in assets under management, and Ron was named one of the top financial advisors in the country by *Barron's* magazine.

When growth began to plateau, Ron and his team implemented the MAKE BIG HAPPEN SYSTEM, setting an aggressive HOT and adopting the MAKE BIG HAPPEN RHYTHMS. As Ron set BIG goal after BIG goal, he continuously asked himself, "What do I have to do to reinvent myself?" just as he did when he pivoted the company away from slipping into oblivion.

When it became clear that one of Ron's blind spots was managing people, we asked, "What do you have to do?" while keeping top of mind the mission he wanted to achieve. He learned the axiom "Hire the best people you can find and get out of their way." So, we focused on hiring senior leaders to manage their areas of expertise while allowing Ron to focus on what he did best: vision and strategy.

By frequently returning to the MAKE BIG HAPPEN QUESTIONS, Ron successfully realized what he needed to do again and again. At one point he deployed revenue-planning tools to change his business model. Another time he partnered with other large institutional partners who could leverage Carson Group's unique resources. Out of a planning session came the initiative to reorganize his firm into three divisions. Each strategic decision led to explosive growth, and each one was an outgrowth of asking the simple question "What do you have to do?"

Since we began working with Carson Group a decade ago, the company has grown more than ten times and now has over $16 billion in assets under management. Ron uses his continued success and influence to give back, having founded the Dreamweaver Foundation, a nonprofit organization dedicated to fulfilling end-of-life dreams for seniors with terminal illnesses. Next stop on Ron's journey: $100 billion.

Ron Carson, a Barron's Hall of Fame advisor, Inc. 5000
CEO, and wealth management industry trailblazer

Ron had dinner at a local charity event in Omaha, Nebraska,
and had the chance to sit with Warren Buffett for several hours, sharing secrets of
their success.

Ron pictured with one of his favorite quotes—a mantra that has taken him from
the childhood farm to financial services fame.

We are often asked how these extraordinary leaders, and hundreds more whom we know, drove their companies to such tremendous success. Certainly, they possessed and exhibited remarkable skills, including entrepreneurship, courage, intellect, determination, and drive. They were also assisted by building and assembling world-class teams, though it is important to note that they did not begin with them.

Dr. Carol Clinton was a former ER doctor on a mission to change her own life and the lives of her patients by founding the nonsurgical medical company Timeless Skin Solutions. Remarkably, she was also a stage 3 ovarian cancer survivor.

When Carol met coach David Sobel, Carol already knew what she wanted—MAKE BIG HAPPEN QUESTION 1 slam dunk! David hopped in and helped Carol establish quarterly and annual planning RHYTHMS and build the action plan to get what she wanted—swish, another slam dunk with MAKE BIG HAPPEN QUESTION 2.

Before long, Carol had adopted the MAKE BIG HAPPEN SYSTEM to a tee. As the business grew, David and Carol kept a close eye on MAKE BIG HAPPEN QUESTION 3: "What could get in the way?"

Carol had left the ER in the first place because she yearned to move on from the high-pressure nature of the job. However, she still had a strong passion to bring personal care to her patients at Timeless Skin Solutions, so she was still spending most of her time in front of her patients.

Carol was also the primary rainmaker of the company, with her feet on the ground hustling to drive new business. While her passion for her work was admirable, David knew the doctor's best intentions were the answer to MAKE BIG HAPPEN QUESTION 3. A CEO spending most of their time with customers would surely get in the way of being able to grow the business in the long term.

David and Carol spoke candidly, and together they made some tough decisions. Carol resolved to shift her time to fulfilling the responsibilities she should be focusing on as CEO, knowing that it was necessary to achieve what she wanted. Fortunately, the answer to MAKE BIG HAPPEN QUESTION 4, "How will you hold yourself accountable?" had been answered a long time ago—through it all, David stayed right by her side.

Suddenly, Carol's cancer returned, and she was forced to withdraw from leadership for chemotherapy. It became clear that the proactive move for her to step out of her patients' rooms and allow others to take care of them on her behalf may have saved the company. Otherwise, Carol's absence would have crippled Timeless Skin Solution without her there to hold it up.

Carol decided it was time to live her best life. After nearly fifteen years, it was time to step away from the business completely—she had more than earned it.

In MAKE BIG HAPPEN style, Dr. Clinton was rewarded for her time, effort, and rigorous adherence to the MAKE BIG HAPPEN QUESTIONS. In late 2020, Carol successfully exited to a regional dermatology company and reaped the well-earned rewards of a vision well executed.

I'VE GOT
SKIN
IN THE
GAME

DR. CAROL CLINTON | DIFFERENT FACES OF OVARIAN CANCER

Dr. Carol Clinton opens up about "the many faces of ovarian cancer" on her popular podcast.

***

The way brothers Rob and Dave Phillips have run their company Phillips Industries is a glowing example of the power of MAKE BIG HAPPEN QUESTION #3: What could get in the way?

Phillips Industries, a family business founded by Hugh Phillips in 1928, manufactures parts for the trucking industry across the world, including the United States, Mexico, Poland, and China. Through the years, Rob, the fourth generation and current CEO, and Dave, executive vice president, have been great at identifying early signs of big challenges with their operations in the United States related to wage increases, corporate taxation, and employment laws. They identified these issues as potentially getting in the way of achieving what they wanted, and resolved to proactively take serious action to remain market leaders in their industry.

"One of the best things we've gotten out of the MAKE BIG HAPPEN SYSTEM is a set of much better processes for tackling challenges by holding productive leadership discussions with the right people, who know what their responsibilities are and have full ownership of the success of their initiatives," Rob commented.

Out of one planning session came the initiative to move their suppliers, workforce, facilities, and production to Mexico. From experience, they had learned that Mexico had a pool of talented and capable people trained in automotive supply chain management at a low cost and a culture in line with that of their company. They recognized the situation as what it was—a huge opportunity to drastically grow the company—and acted quickly.

"There have been dozens of projects like this one, and our MAKE BIG HAPPEN coach's support has been a game changer. Through strategic planning sessions and the rest of the best-practice business rhythms our coach helped us put in place, we've improved the way we communicate, the speed with which we can address problems, and the quality of our decision-making. The results are vast. It's been really, really great for us," Rob shared.

Along with their passion, integrity, and grit, it has been largely Rob and Dave's mindset of anticipating and addressing roadblocks that could get in the way of their success that has allowed Phillips Industries to continue to thrive through the test of time.

Brothers and leaders Rob and Dave Phillips inside one of their highly efficient Phillips Industries production facilities

CEOs are self-motivated, results focused, driven, and independent and have a growth mindset. Sometimes, when we think about accountability, we might ask, "Why would a remarkably successful CEO need accountability?" It is often said that being a CEO can be lonely. If you want to think through something or have someone challenge you, do you talk to your family, your direct reports, or your board? The best players in the world have

> The best players in the world have coaches.

coaches, and through them they can optimize their performance. That is precisely what Patrick Richard did as the CEO and founder of real estate investment firm Stoneweg US. Patrick is remarkably successful in his own right. But by partnering with a coach, he is now able to implement business rhythms that align and accelerate.

Patrick commented, "We started with a planning session to define and align our 2025 vision, our stakeholders, and our culture. From there, we worked backward to what success looks like this year and then this quarter. With that planning in place, we maintain accountability through biweekly meetings with the coach, weekly meetings with the ELT, weekly one-on-ones, executive coaching of the leadership team, and a quarterly planning rhythm. Once we are directionally aligned and lay the tracks through our roadmap process, we can exponentially accelerate performance. As a foreign CEO, I benefit significantly from my coach to better understand the business culture in the United States. Stoneweg US is on an accelerated path to growing investments and building communities as a real estate investment leader."

Rick Weber joined CBC Credit Union as chief financial officer in 2017, and things were not going so well in the business. Rick got straight to work, and by 2019, the credit union had made some progress, but the company was still losing a ton of money, and stress was high. So high that things took an unexpected and life-changing turn: the CEO went into cardiac arrest in front of the entire team in a heated meeting.

Naturally, the CEO took a temporary leave from the business to recover, and Rick stepped in as interim CEO.

That temporary leave stretched out and stretched out until ultimately the doctor ordered the CEO to step away from the business permanently.

On March 1, 2020, Rick officially accepted the full-time position of CEO. Ten days later, the VP of finance, who was supposed to take over the CFO role Rick was leaving, announced she would be taking a five-month maternity leave. A week later, the pandemic started.

"I didn't even know what to think," Rick explains. "We lost a ton of money in the first quarter. It was just a terrible tailspin. We had these explosive meetings where everyone just piled their fears on top of one another. I didn't really want to be here, and nobody else wanted to." So, Rick reached out to coach Sheldon Harris and asked what he should do. With the MAKE BIG HAPPEN QUESTIONS at the ready, Rick and Sheldon blocked out the mayhem and slowed everything down. What did Rick want? What did he have to do to get there? What exactly was getting in the way? How would he hold himself accountable?

By staying committed to the MAKE BIG HAPPEN RHYTHMS, putting some tools in play, and holding themselves accountable, the new CEO and his leadership team started turning things around. By June they had earned back their Q1 losses and achieved breakeven. "We pushed through the fear that had built up, and we systematically started solving problems," Rick said. "We said, 'We don't have to close.' Let's slow things down. How could we keep this open? How could we do that? And we would talk through the issues with a level head and arrive at solutions."

While Sheldon held Rick accountable for his goals, Rick realized his priority as CEO was to focus on his people. He went to work on the front lines, greeting customers face to face, and his executives did the same, leading to a new morale at the credit union. Rick continued to keep his team focused on a singular vision.

Meanwhile, he worked to make sure every employee felt excitement instead of anxiety when they came into work. Rick created an environment that drowned out any fear the news was feeding them, even going so far as to throw a Halloween party with a costume contest. "We never stopped celebrating. We kept our Employee of the Month program, we wore T-shirts with our mascot wearing a cape and called ourselves CBC Heroes, and I think that Halloween party was a real game changer. I have never in my life ever worn a costume, and I said, 'You know what, I need to do something big. I need to blow everyone away.' And everyone just cracked up."

By the end of 2020, CBC Federal Credit Union had its greatest earnings year in its sixty-eight-year history and grew more accounts than ever before.

"I never thought we'd be here in my wildest dreams," Rick says. "You know, I wasn't trying to break records or grow big or do anything fancy. I was just trying to survive. But because we stuck with the discipline of the MAKE BIG HAPPEN SYSTEM, we kept the right things in focus. We made the right decisions, and we kept discipline as a team. We kept it going. And as a result, we're doing fantastic."

CBC Federal Credit Union CEO Rick Weber (left) and his chicken-suited CXO keep morale up in the company's branches by showing off their outrageous Halloween costumes.

As observers and participants in all these success stories, we know that they all possessed an unswerving commitment to a system built on a methodology that accentuates several key traits:

- An unwavering commitment to healthy business RHYTHMS

- A mastery of applying the MAKE BIG HAPPEN QUESTIONS

- A culture of accountability

- Access to world-class tools for running their business

- A rationalized system structured to emphasize earning and generate what Jim Collins would call a "flywheel effect" of ever-growing momentum

These leaders began by identifying a long-term, life-changing outcome that we like to call a "Huge Outrageous Target," or "HOT"—for example, "We doubled the size of our business in three years, from $X to $Y." They further defined the specific and measurable result that would make them celebrate twelve months from now, because they achieved the first milestone of their tremendous journey. They outlined where they needed to be three months from the start, to give them confidence that they would reach their twelve-month outcome, and they did this *every three months*. Through rigorous strategic planning and quarterly reviews, they identified the leading activities that produced the first-quarter outcome and therefore led to the one-year and long-term results. They built systems to track and measure the impact of these actions and to allow themselves to be held accountable to both their commitments and the outcomes they intended to produce. Ultimately, by adhering to these practices, they identified the correct actions at each stage of growth; they avoided the biggest pitfalls, pivoted from mistaken good-faith assumptions and unforeseeable setbacks, and eluded "shiny objects"; and ultimately, they generated tremendous year-over-year growth.

By following the MAKE BIG HAPPEN RHYTHMS and challenging your thinking by the continuous application of the MAKE BIG HAPPEN QUESTIONS, you, too, can MAKE BIG HAPPEN. Now, let's look at over twenty-five tools that will help you through your journey.

CHAPTER 3

Leverage the Proven MAKE BIG HAPPEN TOOLS to Accelerate Your Success

MAKE BIG HAPPEN SYSTEM: Element 3—Leverage the MAKE BIG HAPPEN TOOLS

You cannot mandate productivity; you must provide the tools to let people become their best.

—STEVE JOBS

In the previous chapters, we outlined the foundation of the MAKE BIG HAPPEN SYSTEM that permits discovery and definition and sets into motion an ongoing process of continuous learning, flywheel momentum, and accountability. The MAKE BIG HAPPEN SYSTEM is driven by a series of carefully structured, expertly facilitated business rhythms held at a deliberate frequency and cadence.

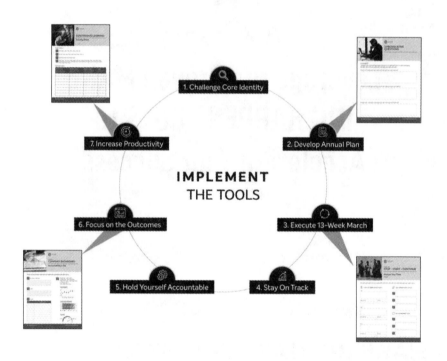

Many other business systems also dictate regular meetings with specified formats, but they lack a key element that produces extraordinary outcomes. Among the most important value adds of the MAKE BIG HAPPEN SYSTEM is the large selection of specialty MAKE BIG HAPPEN TOOLS that allows you to combine strategy with action. Plainly stated, all the magic is in our MAKE BIG HAPPEN TOOLS and their application to your specific circumstances as you navigate through the MAKE BIG HAPPEN RHYTHMS.

BUSINESS RHYTHM MAPPING

Each tool is presented on the following pages in the order they appeared in the MAKE BIG HAPPEN RHYTHMS. However, one tool may be applicable to several rhythms. Therefore, we have mapped each tool to their most applicable MAKE BIG HAPPEN RHYTHM(S) in the table below. We have also included an index at the end of the book that identifies every reference to each tool within the book so you can explore how the tools are used within the context of the MAKE BIG HAPPEN RHYTHMS.

Download an electronic version of the tools at:
www.ceocoaching.com/MakingBigHappen.

TOOL	Reference Page	BUSINESS RHYTHM						
		1. Challenge Core Identity	2. Develop an Annual Plan	3. Execute a 13-Week March	4. Stay on Track	5. Hold Yourself Accountable	6. Focus on the Outcomes	7. Increase Productivity
Vision Worksheet	223	✓						
Mission Worksheet	225	✓						
Core Values Builder	227	✓						
Culture Survey	229	✓						
Unique Value Proposition Identifier	231	✓						
HOT Trajectory Tool	233	✓						
Organization of the Future	235	✓				✓		
Crystal Ball	237		✓			✓		
Annual/Quarterly Planning Session Pre-Work	239		✓	✓				
Secret Ballot	241		✓	✓				
Provocative Questions	243		✓					
Stop-Start-Continue	245		✓	✓		✓		
Acquisition Growth Map	247		✓			✓		
Sales Roadmap, Plan, and Playbook	249		✓					

TOOL	Reference Page	1. Challenge Core Identity	2. Develop an Annual Plan	3. Execute a 13-Week March	4. Stay on Track	5. Hold Yourself Accountable	6. Focus on the Outcomes	7. Increase Productivity
BUSINESS RHYTHM								
Strategic Roadmap	251	✓				✓		
Company Dashboard	253		✓	✓	✓	✓	✓	
Who-What-When	255		✓	✓	✓	✓	✓	
Topgrading Exercise	257			✓		✓		
Initiative Charter	259			✓				
Leading-Lagging Indicators Sequence	261			✓				
Monthly Financial Review Checklist	263				✓	✓		
Goal Scoreboard	265					✓	✓	
Initiative Commitments Tracker	267					✓	✓	
Candidate Evaluation Checklist	269					✓		✓
Interview Scoring Matrix	271					✓		✓
Leadership Team 360° Review	273							✓
Power Hour Planner	275					✓		✓
Continuous Learning Tracking Sheet	277					✓		✓

VISION WORKSHEET

Purpose

The Vision Worksheet provides a simple structure and various examples to make it easy to build a meaningful vision statement for your company.

Instructions

Identify which time frame, key component, and target goal are most appropriate for your company's vision. After deciding on each piece, put them together and write down your vision statement.

Tips

Make sure the time frame you select is foreseeable and realistic. The key component you choose should be especially relevant to the success of your business. Lastly, think BIG—set a target goal that is ambitious and inspirational.

 CEO COACHING
International

VISION
WORKSHEET

1 FIRST, SET A
TIMEFRAME

EXAMPLES:
3, 5 or 10 Years
Stated as a Future Year
i.e. "By 2030"

CONSIDERATIONS
Speed of Industry Change
Market Growth Maturity
Intensity of Competition
Desire to Exit the Business
Capital Needs & Sources

YOUR COMPANY:

2 NEXT, ADD THE
KEY COMPONENT

EXAMPLES:
Revenue
Profit/EBITDA
Sales Volume
Capitalization
Valuation
Customers
Product Portfolio
Employee Size
Business Locations
Geographic Markets

YOUR COMPANY:

3 LASTLY, DEFINE YOUR
TARGET GOAL

EXAMPLES:
$212,000,000
3 granola varieties
5 Countries
USA, Canada and China
20 yearly deals
7,500 unique user accounts

YOUR COMPANY:

4 NOW PUT THE ELEMENTS TOGETHER TO CREATE YOUR
VISION STATEMENT

EXAMPLE: By **2028**, we will be serving **60,000,000** customers across **5 different countries** with a **full line of sports apparel** for extreme athletes.

info@ceocoaching.com   ceocoachinginternational.com

MISSION WORKSHEET

Purpose

The Mission Worksheet makes it easy to build a powerful mission statement for your company.

Instructions

Answer the four questions in the template. Then, take a step back and ask yourself if those answers meet all the criteria of a strong and sound mission statement described in MAKE BIG HAPPEN RHYTHM 1. If not, adjust your statement until it is perfect.

Tips

Remember that a vision statement tells your team where you are going in terms of growth in the future, whereas a mission statement should be focused on the present and tell your team and the rest of the world why what you do matters.

MISSION
WORKSHEET

CEO COACHING
International

WHAT
CUSTOMER BENEFIT

WHO
POTENTIAL MARKET

HOW
PRODUCT SERVICE

WHY
ULTIMATE PURPOSE

BUILD YOUR MISSION STATEMENT

EXAMPLE:
Our mission is to remove the roadblocks to investing for all investors by creating an easy-to-use technology platform with low account minimums so every person can reach financial freedom.

Our mission is to

1. DO WHAT

For

2. WHO ARE YOU DOING IT FOR

By

3. HOW YOU DO IT

So

4. WHY YOU DO IT

TEST IT

☐ Is it timeless?

☐ Does it contribute to your personal life mission as CEO?

☐ Is it consistent with your company's values?

☐ Does it help your leadership team make decisions?

☐ Does it energize your employees?

CORE VALUES BUILDER

Purpose

Having strong core values attracts better employees, increases resilience in your team, and provides guidelines for making decisions. The Core Values Builder provides an easy-to-use framework to determine your organization's core values if you have not established them yet.

Instructions

Place a check mark next to the values in the word bank that you want your company to exhibit. Then review the selected words and circle your top ten. Rank each of the top ten in order and include as many as necessary in your core values. Commit to communicating and living those core values every day.

> Core values are only useful if they are thoughtfully developed, ingrained, and embodied by an organization.

Tips

Core values are only useful if they are thoughtfully developed, ingrained, and embodied by an organization. Do not think of this as just another box to check in the process of building a company; instead, realize that your core values are a critical determinant of the type of company you are building. To this end, be sure to utilize your core values during the interview process when making hiring decisions and during the performance review process when considering promotions.

EXERCISE
CORE VALUES BUILDER

EXERCISE
CORE VALUES BUILDER

STEP 1 Place a check mark next to the values that you want your company to represent.

STEP 1 *Continued* Place a check mark next to the values that you want your company to represent.

CEO COACHING
International

EXERCISE
CORE VALUES BUILDER

STEP 2 Go back over the checked values and circle your top 10.

Ask yourself the following questions to narrow down the list to find your values:

1. What values feel far more important than the others?
2. What traits in others annoy you? (turn this around and there is usually a value underneath it)
3. What values would you be saddened to hear others say you don't demonstrate?

STEP 3 Determine your company's core values.

Write down the list of 10 top values in the sheet below and rate each one on a scale of 1 to 10 where 1 is somewhat important to you and 10 is it's passionately important to you. Using the scores, boil down the list of ten to those that clearly stand out from the rest. Between 3 and 7 values is typically optimal.

VALUE	IMPORTANCE →	SOMEWHAT				VERY			PASSIONATELY		
		1	2	3	4	5	6	7	8	9	10
		1	2	3	4	5	6	7	8	9	10
		1	2	3	4	5	6	7	8	9	10
		1	2	3	4	5	6	7	8	9	10
		1	2	3	4	5	6	7	8	9	10
		1	2	3	4	5	6	7	8	9	10
		1	2	3	4	5	6	7	8	9	10
		1	2	3	4	5	6	7	8	9	10
		1	2	3	4	5	6	7	8	9	10

STEP 4 Live your life and run your business by your values!

Communicate your values to your whole team. Do not change them frequently. Reinforce that these are the values that you want your company to embody. Incentivize others to live your core values through nominations and awards. Filter or screen people, events and surprises that come into your life through your values. When you face a challenge, use your core values as a compass to make decisions. You will have no regrets, whatever happens, when you make a decision that stays true to your values.

info@ceocoaching.com

ceocoachinginternational.com

CULTURE SURVEY

Purpose

The Culture Survey allows a CEO and the leadership team to determine the strengths and weaknesses in their company's culture as reported by their employees.

Instructions

Have your team answer the questions to evaluate eight key areas of your company's culture. Convert that feedback into an action plan for refining your culture.

Tips

As you ask others to take the survey, set the expectation that you are looking for honest answers, not what they think the CEO wants to hear. Have employees submit survey responses electronically so that the data can be automatically tabulated.

 CEO COACHING
international

CULTURE SURVEY

INSTRUCTIONS

STEP 1 Have all employees take the survey anonymously.

STEP 2 Discuss the input with your team to identify gaps in your current culture compared to your ideal culture.

STEP 3 Develop new initiatives with clear deadlines as needed to improve the weaknesses.

STEP 4 Have your employees take it every year to keep your finger on the pulse and continually improve your culture.

THE SURVEY

CATEGORY	QUESTION	SCORE (1-10)
VISION	Is it clear and compelling?	
	Is the company aligned around it?	
MISSION	Is it authentic?	
	It is meaningful?	
CORE VALUES	How well do we live them out?	
	Do they guide our decisions?	
HOTs	Are they important?	
	Do we know why they're important?	
UNIQUE VALUE PROPOSITION	Is it significant?	
	Are we faithful to it?	
TEAM	Do we have the right people?	
	Are they in the right seats?	
COMMUNICATION	Is it clear and efficient?	
	Are we transparent and accessible?	
ACCOUNTABILITY	Do we measure our results?	
	Do we do what we say we're going to do?	

info@ceocoaching.com   ceocoachinginternational.com

UNIQUE VALUE PROPOSITION IDENTIFIER

Purpose

The Unique Value Proposition Identifier helps you clarify the product and service attributes that are most important to your customers.

Instructions

List and rank the aspects of your offering that customers appreciate the most. This will help you identify where your company can outperform the competition in those areas that are most important to your customers or clients.

Tips

Do not do this exercise alone. An effective unique value proposition must be completed in a collaborative manner. Make sure you discuss, debate, and align with your team.

UNIQUE VALUE PROPOSITION IDENTIFIER

A unique value proposition (UVP) defines the problem you solve, who benefits from the solution, and how they derive the benefits. It is unique to your business and answers the question of why your customers or clients should pick you over your competitors.

STEP 1 Secondary Research

- Explore industry journals, associations & leading orgs, magazines, online articles to discover trends in your industry. Follow your hunches and track down reliable and compelling data. Ask yourself:
  - ☐ Where are the areas of growth opportunity?
  - ☐ What are the potential opportunities to differentiate, disrupt or create your own niche?
  - ☐ What are your most successful competitors doing that makes them unique in the eyes of your customers?

STEP 2 Primary Research

- Go out and interview customers, prospects and experts. The ideas you receive will help you find patterns, discover opportunities, and determine where to focus your attention. Ask them:
  - ☐ Why do you buy from us? From our competitors?
  - ☐ What are you not getting in the product or service that you wish you could get?
  - ☐ What are the aspects of the product or service that you value most?
  - ☐ What 1 – 2 unique things could we offer that would make you purchase from us every time?

STEP 3 Apply the Findings to Your Company

- List the top 5 criteria that you believe make up your UVP. Discuss, debate, and align with your team.
- Ask your customers, prospects and employees for their input as well. How do they differ from your own team's conclusions? What have you not yet considered and what might need changing?

STEP 4 Evaluate the Competition

- Rank your competition on a scale of 1-10 on the same criteria to identify your opportunity to outperform the competition or widen the gap between you and them.

	Criteria # 1	Criteria # 2	Criteria # 3	Criteria # 4	Criteria # 5
You					
Competitor 1					
Competitor 2					
Competitor 3					

STEP 5 Identify and Prove Your Unique Value Proposition

- Determine where you have or can create a competitive advantage. This gap or wedge in the criteria you rank highly on compared to your competitors gives you the room to leverage a UVP and be the company your competitors choose every time.
- How can we prove the UVP we identified? We must be able to back it up with data, customer testimonials and/or facts.
- Create a plan to translate the new or revised UVP into your internal and external communication and branding. Consider your website, marketing collateral, packaging, internal sales training, client communications, etc.

info@ceocoaching.com   ceocoachinginternational.com

HOT TRAJECTORY TOOL

Purpose

The HOT Trajectory Tool helps you break down a HOT (Huge Outrageous Target) into a series of five annual milestones.

Instructions

Determine your HOT and its time frame, up to five years. Then work backward year by year to confirm the target that you need to hit each year to stay on track.

Tips

Do not set your HOT arbitrarily. Strong HOTs are SMART[9]—*s*pecific, *m*easurable, *a*ttainable, *r*elevant, and *t*ime bound. Review the "Factors" list on the tool when determining the rate of growth.

---

9   G. T. Doran, "There's a S.M.A.R.T. way to write management's goals and objectives," *Management Review*, 1981, *70*(11), 35–36.

THE HOT TRAJECTORY TOOL

STEP 1 Set your long-term HOT.

STEP 2 Identify the possible factors that are likely to influence the trajectory of your indicators.

STEP 3 Once you have selected your growth trajectory, identify the specific, year-by-year numbers that will allow your company to reach its long-term HOT.

THIS YEAR ←	1-YEAR HOT ←			LONG TERM HOT
YEAR 1 Ex: Revenue $30mm	**YEAR 2** Ex: Revenue $40mm	**YEAR 3** Ex: Revenue $55mm	**YEAR 4** Ex: Revenue $70mm	**YEAR 5** Ex: Revenue $90mm

FACTORS THAT INFLUENCE HOT TRAJECTORY

NETWORK EFFECTS	Network effects mean that as more customers use your product or service, the product or service becomes more valuable to everybody else using it.
RETAINED EARNINGS	The more you reinvest, the faster you should expect to grow.
LIFECYCLE STAGE	Early-stage companies might grow fast while older companies with mature products might flatline without innovation.
INDUSTRY GROWTH	Which growth pattern, linear, increasing, decreasing, or S-shaped, best describes your industry?
MARKETING EXPENDITURES	Are you planning to maintain, increase, or decrease your marketing expenditures over time?
BUSINESS CAPACITY	If your business is not easily scalable, expect revenue growth to decrease as you approach the capacity limit, unless you can promptly plan for capacity expansion.
CHURN RATE	Churn rates move the needle in the opposite direction of growth. Lower churn rates lead to higher growth trajectories.

ORGANIZATION OF THE FUTURE

Purpose

The Organization of the Future tool challenges you to define what your ideal organization will look like several years from now, assuming you have achieved your HOT. It is a disruptive way of looking at your organization. Its purpose is to challenge you to accelerate key hires and upgrades now, because having these individuals on your team will make it easier for you to achieve your HOT.

Instructions

Create an org chart by title and function, representing your ideal leadership team at the time your HOT is achieved. Summarize the ideal profile of each member.

Tips

When drafting the chart and the ideal profile, ask yourself, "What are the biggest unanswered questions that I have on the road to my HOT? What is the title, function, and profile of the person whose experience has already allowed them to answer those questions?"

ORGANIZATION OF THE FUTURE

STEP 1

Sketch the organizational structure that is necessary to achieve your long-term HOT. Focus on the roles required rather than the people that will fill them.

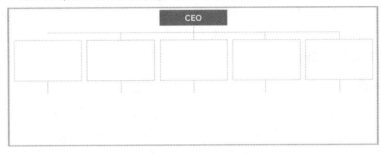

STEP 2

For each position in the org chart, map out the following key considerations to prepare for an effective recruiting and hiring process.

ROLE	NECESSARY EXPERIENCE Ex: Managing sales teams in foreign markets; Enabling acquisitions	PROBABLE CHALLENGES Ex: Long lead times for overseas engineering; Supply chain inefficiencies	POTENTIAL OPPORTUNITIES Ex: Renegotiating lines of credit to free up cash; Being first to market	ANTICIPATED CONSTRAINTS Ex: Bureaucratic customer service culture; Traditional bank lending agreements

CRYSTAL BALL

Purpose

The Crystal Ball exercise helps you determine what you want to accomplish, and provides clarity on the activities that lead to your desired outcomes.

Instructions

Imagine it is one year in the future. You and your team are celebrating your huge success. Ask yourself what accomplishments you are celebrating. Then, what are the specific and measurable activities that you executed daily, weekly, monthly, and quarterly that produced those BIG goals?

Tips

Make sure your outcomes in step 1 are specific and measurable and that your activities in step 2 are activities instead of restated outcomes. For example, the answer in step 2 to "I grew the business by 50 percent" cannot be "I got more customers." Rather, it should list the activities you performed to gain more customers.

EXERCISE
THE CRYSTAL BALL®

You look into a Crystal Ball® and can see into the future to the end of next year. A great year is ahead of you! Write down what you see.

STEP 1

The year you envisioned has now come and gone. We are celebrating the year because we achieved the following specific and measurable outcomes.

STEP 2

For each of the three outcomes above, what are the top two specific and measurable activities you executed that made you achieve that outcome?

ANNUAL/QUARTERLY PLANNING SESSION PRE-WORK

Purpose

Completing this Annual/Quarterly Planning Session Pre-Work exercise amplifies the productivity of an annual or quarterly planning session. This homework collects the perspectives of your leadership team on the most critical questions, laying the groundwork for your planning session.

Instructions

Ask all planning session participants to complete the exercise in advance of the session. After receiving all responses, anonymize and consolidate all the answers to each question. Bring the aggregated pre-work to the planning session.

Tips

Merge similar comments and count the frequency of multiple occurrences to indicate how common the response was.

ANNUAL PLANNING SESSION
PRE-WORK

Answer the following questions from the perspective of the company as a whole.

REFLECT - Over the past 12 months:	
What went **right**?	
What went **wrong**?	
What did we **learn**?	

ANALYZE - How did we do:	
On our **annual goals** compared to how we said we would do?	
On the **specific and measurable activities** we've been tracking because they'll lead to the outcome we want?	

ANTICIPATE - In the next year:	
What are our greatest **opportunities**?	
What are our greatest **challenges**?	
What is the **#1 goal** we could achieve that would have the biggest impact on our growth?	

info@ceocoaching.com   ceocoachinginternational.com

QUARTERLY ALIGNMENT SESSION
PRE-WORK

Answer the following questions from the perspective of the company as a whole.

REFLECT - Over the past 90 days:	
What went **right**?	
What went **wrong**?	
What did we **learn**?	

ANALYZE - How did we do:	
On our **quarterly goals** compared to how we said we would do?	
On the **specific and measurable activities** we've been tracking because they'll lead to the outcome we want?	

ANTICIPATE - In the next quarter:	
What are our greatest **opportunities**?	
What are our greatest **challenges**?	
What is the **#1 goal** we could achieve that would have the biggest impact on our growth?	

info@ceocoaching.com   ceocoachinginternational.com

SECRET BALLOT

Purpose

The Secret Ballot helps leadership teams discover the company's weaknesses and areas of misalignment.

Instructions

Distribute a blank Secret Ballot to each member of your leadership team during a planning session. Give them several minutes to fill it out and return it. Shuffle up the slips and read out the scores to the whole group one at a time while someone tallies the numbers. Unpack the results together immediately.

Tips

The Secret Ballot must be filled out and submitted anonymously to receive meaningful responses.

SECRET BALLOT

Too many companies never take a moment to nail down what they've done right, what they've done wrong and what they learned. As a result, they are destined to continue bad habits and make poor decisions.

Distribute the Secret Ballot to your team members. Collect the responses anonymously.
Discover areas of misalignment and room for improvement.

THE SURVEY

QUESTION	Score (1-10)
How well do we communicate our vision?	
How well do we live our core values?	
How satisfied are you in your current position?	
How strong is our management team?	
How likely are we to succeed at our strategy?	
How well do we internally communicate as a company?	

WHAT IS OUR WEAKEST LINK?

WHAT IS THE #1 PROBLEM WE NEED TO ADDRESS RIGHT NOW?

IS THERE SOMETHING THAT WE'RE IGNORING THE OBVIOUS ABOUT?

info@ceocoaching.com   ceocoachinginternational.com

PROVOCATIVE QUESTIONS

Purpose

The Provocative Questions tool can help you completely reinvent your company and ensure you stay one step ahead of any competitor or new technology that could threaten your business.

> **Stay one step ahead of any competitor or new technology that could threaten your business.**

Instructions

Imagine that you are starting a brand-new company to compete with your current one. Write down one to three answers for each question in the template. When you are done, step back and decide which of the tactics in the hypothetical scenario you will commit to doing.

Tips

It is not uncommon to look at your responses to the Provocative Questions and say, "We want to be like that company instead." This is the point of the exercise. Build the company of your dreams!

3 PROVOCATIVE QUESTIONS

SCENARIO

Imagine you are starting a new company to compete with your current company. Answer these three questions to design your new company.

What am I doing now that I would stop doing in my new company?

What am I not doing now that I would start doing in my new company?

How would I compete to try to put my old company out of business?

STOP-START-CONTINUE

Purpose

The Stop-Start-Continue tool helps leaders regain focus on their high-payoff activities (HPA)—the most important activities to focus on to MAKE BIG HAPPEN.

Instructions

Determine the top three activities that take up your time but will not lead to the outcomes you want to achieve and are therefore getting in your way. Then, determine the activities that you are not currently doing that would have a huge impact on your business. Resolve to start doing those. Lastly, make note of which activities are critical and which you should continue doing.

Tips

Top CEOs focus their time on only five things: vision, cash, people, key relationships, and learning. Anything on your agenda that does not fall into one of those categories is probably not a good use of your time.

EXERCISE
STOP – START – CONTINUE

Use this tool to start spending 90% of your time on the 10% of activities that lead to your highest results.

☐ I NEED TO **STOP** DOING THESE:

STOP:

DELEGATE TO: BY DATE:

STOP:

DELEGATE TO: BY DATE:

STOP:

DELEGATE TO: BY DATE:

▷ I WILL **START** DOING THESE:

1

2

3

⟫ I WILL **CONTINUE** THESE:

1

2

3

ACQUISITION GROWTH MAP

Purpose

You can get far down the road to your goal via organic growth alone, but the acquisition of a competitive or complementary business will certainly help you achieve your goal faster. The Acquisition Growth Map helps you analyze the impact of one or more acquisitions on the attainment of your HOT.

Instructions

Fill out the template as if you planned to achieve your HOT solely via organic growth, with predicted annual growth rates. Then, test hypothetical scenarios involving the acquisition of one or more firms over the same period, mixed with organic growth. Evaluate the attractiveness of these acquisitions as a possible course toward achieving your HOT.

Tips

Consider your Cash Bridge and Cash Bridge Dashboard when deciding whether acquisitions make financial sense for your business.

ACQUISITION GROWTH MAP

Template

	STARTING REV	GROWTH	GROWTH $	ENDING REV	ACQUISITION	ENDING REV
2021	$ -	0%	$ -	$ -	+ $ -	= $ -
2022	$ -	0%	$ -	$ -	+ $ -	= $ -
2023	$ -	0%	$ -	$ -	+ $ -	= $ -
2024	$ -	0%	$ -	$ -	+ $ -	= $ -
2025	$ -	0%	$ -	$ -	$ -	$ -

Examples

0 Acquisitions

	STARTING REV	GROWTH	GROWTH $	ENDING REV
2021	$ 42,500,060	25%	$ 10,625,015	$ 53,125,075
2022	$ 53,125,075	25%	$ 13,281,269	$ 66,406,344
2023	$ 66,406,344	25%	$ 16,601,586	$ 83,007,930
2024	$ 83,007,930	25%	$ 20,751,982	$ 103,759,912
2025	$ 103,759,912	25%	$ 25,939,978	$ 129,699,890

1 Acquisition

	STARTING REV	GROWTH	GROWTH $	SUBTOTAL	ACQUISITION	ENDING REV
2021	$ 42,500,060	25%	$ 10,625,015	$ 53,125,075 +	=	$ 53,125,075
2022	$ 53,125,075	25%	$ 13,281,269	$ 66,406,344 =	$ 20,000,000 =	$ 86,406,344
2023	$ 86,406,344	25%	$ 21,601,586	$ 108,007,930 +	=	$ 108,007,930
2024	$ 108,007,930	25%	$ 27,001,982	$ 135,009,912 +	=	$ 135,009,912
2025	$ 135,009,912	25%	$ 33,752,478	$ 168,762,390		$ 168,762,390

2 Acquisitions

	STARTING REV	GROWTH	GROWTH $	SUBTOTAL	ACQUISITION	ENDING REV
2021	$ 42,500,060	25%	$ 10,625,015	$ 53,125,075 +	=	$ 53,125,075
2022	$ 53,125,075	25%	$ 13,281,269	$ 66,406,344 +	$ 20,000,000 =	$ 86,406,344
2023	$ 86,406,344	25%	$ 21,601,586	$ 108,007,930 +	$ 20,000,000 =	$ 128,007,930
2024	$ 128,007,930	25%	$ 32,001,982	$ 160,009,912 +	=	$ 160,009,912
2025	$ 160,009,912	25%	$ 40,002,478	$ 200,012,390		$ 200,012,390

4 Acquisitions

	STARTING REV	GROWTH	GROWTH $	SUBTOTAL	ACQUISITION	ENDING REV
2021	$ 42,500,060	25%	$ 10,625,015	$ 53,125,075 +	=	$ 53,125,075
2022	$ 53,125,075	25%	$ 13,281,269	$ 66,406,344 +	$ 20,000,000 =	$ 86,406,344
2023	$ 86,406,344	25%	$ 21,601,586	$ 108,007,930 +	$ 20,000,000 =	$ 128,007,930
2024	$ 128,007,930	25%	$ 32,001,982	$ 160,009,912 +	$ 20,000,000 =	$ 180,009,912
2025	$ 180,009,912	25%	$ 45,002,478	$ 225,012,390	$ 20,000,000	$ 245,012,390

SALES ROADMAP, PLAN, AND PLAYBOOK

Purpose

The Sales Roadmap, Plan, and Playbook (SRPP) enables you to build an actionable sales strategy, including definitions of assumptions pertaining to the clearest path for growth, the specific focus that will guide your sales team, and the particular activities that produce your desired outcome.

Instructions

Fill out the roadmap to outline all the assumptions related to the clearest path to achieving your sales goal. Add specifics to those roadmap assumptions using the plan. Lastly, use the playbook to outline the details of your plan of action, the leading activities in your sales funnel, how your company will perform them, and the method you will use to learn, adjust, and hold the sales team accountable.

Tips

Each component of the Revenue Bridge should have its own SRPP. Taken together, all those SRPPs form the foundation of an executable, winning sales strategy. It can also be used to onboard new salespeople by summarizing the strategy and giving them all the information they need in order to win.

SALES ROADMAP, PLAN AND PLAYBOOK

Roadmap Worksheet
Map and Quantify the Key Assumptions of your Revenue Growth Target

REVENUE GROWTH TARGET:
CURRENT $0

From Existing Customers: $_____
PLAN

From New Customers: $_____
PLAN

Expected Customer Attrition: $_____

KEY ASSUMPTIONS FOR GROWTH FROM EXISTING CUSTOMERS
E.G.

Increase ATV (Average Transaction Value) from $____ to $____ on ____% of customers

____% of customers will accept price increases of ____%

Sell $____ in newly launched products

Upsell $____ by selling add-on Products or Services

KEY ASSUMPTIONS FOR GROWTH FROM NEW CUSTOMERS
E.G.

Ideal Customer generates $_____ per year

I need ____# of new "Ideal Customers"

Based on Sales Cycles & Payment Schedules, we need:
____# in Q1 ____# in Q2 ____# in Q3 ____# in Q4

Plan Worksheet
Define the Specifics behind each Roadmap Assumption
"These Products," "These Customers," "These Territories," etc.

E.G., UPSELL $_____ VIA ADD-ON PRODUCTS OR SERVICES
THESE SPECIFIC CUSTOMERS OR THIS PRODUCT OR CUSTOMERS

ALREADY BUYS PRODUCT/SERVICE A & COULD LIKELY ALSO BUY PRODUCT B:

A: _____ B: _____

AND WE WOULD NEED THIS TARGET'S ____% OF THEM PURCHASED IT

E.g., SIGN ____# of NEW CUSTOMERS OF "IDEAL PROFILE" PER QTR.
WE WILL FOCUS ON THESE NAMED CUSTOMERS OR CLASSES OF CUSTOMER:

WE WILL FOCUS ON NEW CUSTOMER ACQUISITIONS IN THESE TERRITORIES:

WILL BE FOCUS ON THIS OR THESE PRODUCTS TO THOSE CUSTOMERS

SALES ROADMAP, PLAN AND PLAYBOOK

Plan Worksheet: Activities
Identify the type and frequency of leading key leading activities in your sales funnel

Live Conversations with Qualified Leads

Meetings / Presentations

Quotes Issued

New Customers

E.g., NEW CLIENT ACQUISITIONS
Working backwards from the # of New "Ideal" Customers that you need to add per quarter, based on your Roadmap and Plan:

1. How many quotes do you need to issue to give you confidence that you will close that # of customers?

2. How many presentations do you need to give to issue that many quotes?

3. How many live conversations with qualified prospects must you build, to have that many opportunities to present?

Adjust the funnel to match your sales process. Add, subtract or rename stages as necessary.

Plan Worksheet: Script
Define the best practices to guide your salespeople's performance of those activities

CONVERSATION TO MEETING

1 INTRO
WHO YOU ARE. KEEP IT BRIEF AND GO STRAIGHT TO THE ATTENTION GETTER
"Hello, I'm XXXX with MyCo."

2 ATTENTION GETTER
WHY THEY SHOULD GET TO KNOW YOU
"Our customer told us..."
Every pitch is a conversation worth paying for. [Choose an attention getter based on pre-visit research]
Anticipate likely questions and objections.

3 TEACHABLE MOMENT
AN EXAMPLE TO BACK UP YOUR ATTENTION GETTER
"For example..."
[Choose teachable moment that matches your attention getter & pre-visit research]

4 WIN
"WIN" - TIME TO PLAN DEMO AND MAKE A PITCH.
"I'd like to have 30 minutes of your time to..."
[Choose transition to "win" that matches your teachable moment]

DEFINING THE SCRIPT
Complete the exercise for each conversion phase in the funnel
(e.g., Conversation to Scheduled Meeting, Quote to Closed Sale)

1 Define and practice the specific pitch that achieves your desired conversion rate.

3 "Model the Masters" – define the above based on what your top performers or the top performers in the industry do.

2 Anticipate the likeliest questions and likeliest objections, and identify your preferred answers.

4 Role Play and Practice, Practice, Practice.

STRATEGIC ROADMAP

Purpose

Part of the MAKE BIG HAPPEN RHYTHMS is to break down your long-term HOT into annual goals and then divide that annual goal into quarterly milestones and initiatives. This tool helps you build a roadmap of the activities and associated KPIs each quarter that will lead to your goal.

Instructions

Write down your annual goal. Fill in your quarterly initiatives. Measure your KPIs to see if the initiatives are moving the needle toward the goal.

Tips

Do not forget that the fundamental business goal is growth in revenue or EBITDA. Ask yourself what levers will move the company in the right direction and cause that growth goal to be realized.

STRATEGIC ROADMAP

STEP 1

Fill in the annual target that you determined using the HOT Trajectory Tool.

ANNUAL GOAL:

STEP 2

Fill in the quarterly initiatives you determined in the planning session. These should be executable chunks of the annual strategy.

Q1:   Q2:   Q3:   Q4:

STEP 3

Measure KPIs to know if the initiatives are moving the needle toward the goal.

COMPANY DASHBOARD

Purpose

The Company Dashboard is a summary-level display of the company's goals, initiatives, and KPIs. It tracks the metrics that are most critical to your company's success.

Instructions

After determining the key metrics to include in the dashboard, aggregate the data to determine the best way of displaying it visually. Update it regularly. Post it on an intranet portal or even the wall to make sure everyone sees your goals and actual numbers at all times and whether they are winning. If results start to slip, take corrective action.

Tips

Create a more useful, insightful, updated dashboard by using data visualization software online.

EXAMPLE
COMPANY DASHBOARD

Track your key business indicators in a dashboard accessible by the whole team.

STEP 1 Business Indicator

STEP 2 Goal

STEP 3 Track

DATE	Measurement

STEP 4 Automate, optimize and visualize your data using the Make BIG Happen online platform.

Get started today at
www.makeBIGhappen.com.

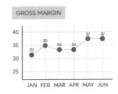

GROSS MARGIN

DAYS SALES OUTSTANDING

APR	27
MAR	28
FEB	30
JAN	31

■ 1-15 Days ■ 16-30 Days ■ 31-60 Days ■ Over 60 Days

REVENUE

WHO-WHAT-WHEN

Purpose

The Who-What-When tracking tool records the action items that team members agree to.

Instructions

During every meeting, designate one participant to record action items in the tracker as they come up. At the end of the meeting, take a few minutes to go over each of the action items and determine who will be responsible for them and by what date.

Tips

Circulate the list after the meeting for accountability. At the next session, pull it up and go over each item to make sure it all got done.

WHO-WHAT-WHEN
TRACKER

CEO COACHING
International

| Who will do what by when? | Use this template to clearly document the "to-do" items that are agreed to in a meeting. |

[Insert Meeting Name]   **[Insert Date]**

WHO	WHAT	WHEN
Owner	Action Item	Deadline

TOPGRADING EXERCISE

Purpose

The Topgrading Exercise brings clarity to the quality of talent on your team by guiding you to grade your employees objectively on the most critical points.

> Grade your employees objectively on the most critical points.

Instructions

Write your employees' names and give them a grade of A, B, or C for each of the two topgrading dimensions: whether they get the work done and how the work gets done.

Tips

To learn more about topgrading, read Geoff Smart and Randy Street's book *Who: A Method for Hiring* and Bradford Smart's book *Topgrading: The Proven Hiring and Promoting Method That Turbocharges Company Performance.*

TOPGRADING EXERCISE

CEO COACHING
International

Topgrading Definitions

Evaluation Areas	A Player	B Player	C Player
Getting The Work Done: RESULTS	A player is someone that **at least 90% of the time**, achieves a level of quality and quantity of work that only the **top 10%** of people in this role could accomplish.	B player is someone that **at least 50%** of the time, achieves a level of quality and quantity of work that only the **top 10%** of people in this role could accomplish.	C player is someone that more **than 50%** of the time, operates at a level below what the top **10%** of people in this role could accomplish.
How the Work is Done: CORE VALUES	Consistently demonstrates **ALL** core values of the Company. In the rare occasion that behavior is not in line with a core value, he/she quickly acts to correct the behavior.	Consistently demonstrates **MOST** core values. May have trouble with **ONE** specific core value and, with proper coaching, can overcome the behavior.	Has trouble demonstrating two or more core values, or behavior within one core value is so outside the expected behavior that coaching is not expected to change the behavior.

Topgrading Results

Employee Name	RESULTS	CORE VALUES	Overall Score

INITIATIVE CHARTER

Purpose

The Initiative Charter is a simple tool for identifying key initiatives and their leading activities, risks, and owners.

Instructions

During a quarterly planning session, identify key initiatives and fill out a charter for each. Review the charters at a key point in the session to prioritize initiatives and confirm which ones to commit to for the quarter.

Tips

When determining key activities, select the top three to five and make sure they have specific and measurable activities that lead to the achievement of the initiative.

CEO COACHING
International

INITIATIVE CHARTER

MEETING:

DATE:

EXECUTIVE SPONSOR:

INITIATIVE QUARTER:

INITIATIVE NAME:

SPECIFIC & MEASURABLE
OUTCOME OF THE INITIATIVE:

Format: From **X** to **Y** by **When**

LEAD (WHO)	ACTIVITY (WHAT)	DUE DATE (WHEN)

KEY ACTIVITIES TO ACHIEVE THE OUTCOME:

RISK	MITIGATION STEPS

info@ceocoaching.com

ceocoachinginternational.com

LEADING-LAGGING INDICATORS SEQUENCE

Purpose

The Leading-Lagging Indicators Sequence helps identify the work to do that will lead to success.

Instructions

Write down your HOT (a lagging indicator) at the top of the tool. Break down the driver of that outcome in a sequential chain of activities (leading indicators) until you find the most actionable root activity.

Tips

Remember, activities that precede a lagging indicator (outcome) are called leading indicators. Continue to work backward until you identify the key leading activity that feeds the leading indicators.

CEO COACHING
International

LEADING–LAGGING INDICATORS SEQUENCE

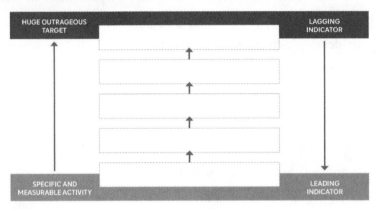

HUGE OUTRAGEOUS TARGET

LAGGING INDICATOR

SPECIFIC AND MEASURABLE ACTIVITY

LEADING INDICATOR

INSTRUCTIONS

STEP 1 Start by writing down your goal in the top box in the flow chart.

STEP 2 Identify what would make that goal achievable and write it in the next box down.

STEP 3 Repeat until you arrive at the specific and measurable activities you can start keeping score on today.

EXAMPLE

Add $5 million in sales

Have $6 million in negotiated contracts

Schedule 200 prospect calls

Make 4,000 cold calls

Hire 5 new sales reps by March

info@ceocoaching.com

ceocoachinginternational.com

MONTHLY FINANCIAL REVIEW CHECKLIST

Purpose

The Monthly Financial Review Checklist helps leaders have the financial information they need to look out the rearview mirror and identify developing trends, while also looking out the windshield to see what is ahead.

Instructions

The checklist provides a review of the monthly financial statements and common financial KPIs, including

- accrual-based financials;

- twelve-month budget, and budget to actual monthly reporting;

- rolling twelve-month forecast; and

- quarterly projections.

It provides guidance for heads of finance to develop reports as well as CEOs to strategize around the reports.

Tips

Our checklist tool is only the starting point. The key is to have access to a quality strategic CFO who can identify issues and find solutions.

MONTHLY FINANCIAL REVIEW CHECKLIST
FOR EXECUTIVE LEADERS

Leadership teams must do a thorough review of financials and consider them in context. Look at the last few months to determine developing trends, comparing to monthly, YTD and prior year actuals. Consider:

1. What is the long-term strategy of the company and what are we doing to get there?
2. What is the best allocation of resources to grow revenues? Is now the right time to hire a...?
3. How do my daily decisions fit into my near-term, mid-term and long-term plans?
   Make sure you consult all three plans whenever you are making a "one change" is your business.

BALANCE SHEET

It is key to evaluate and understand the trends as this can assist in identifying issues and concerns.

☐ Cash Trends - understand what is influencing your changing cash position.
   Are there potential cash shortfalls for the next 12 months that need to be addressed?
   What is causing cash to be tight?

☐ Accounts Receivable
   Can you influence your Days Sales Outstanding to reduce your cash conversion period?
   Do you know what your current AR position is and why/who is delinquent?
   Is there any potential for write-offs and required reserves?
   Should you change terms on your clients to restrict exposure to bad debt?
   Are there any revenue streams that have not been captured and are potential unrecorded receivables?

☐ Accounts Payable
   How can we reduce our Days Payable Outstanding?
   Can you negotiate more favorable terms with Vendors to assist in your cash flow?
   Is there a more efficient process for AP to provide visibility of your payables?

☐ Accrued Expenses
   Are all accruals reflected on the financial reports accurate and up to date?
   Do you potentially have any additional liabilities that have not been recorded?

☐ Assure you are monitoring the required metrics for any covenants the entity is required to achieve?

☐ Working Capital Trends - evaluate trends and consider your future inflows/outflows to assure you have adequate working capital to meet the organization's needs.

INCOME STATEMENT

☐ What steps can be taken to improve profitability?

☐ KPIs -- what is key to your success and should be monitored regularly to identify changes and issues?
   Ex: Revenue Growth, Cost of Sales as a % of Revenue, Gross Margin %, Operating Expenses as % of Sales,
   Net Income %. Many other key indices may be appropriate depending upon your business.

☐ Comparison to Budgets and understanding variances and more importantly, how this will impact your business in the short term and long term so you can plan appropriately.

CASH FLOW STATEMENT

☐ What is influencing your cash trends?

☐ Are there any actions you can take to enhance your cash from operating activities?

☐ How are you managing your nonoperating cashflows?

☐ What are the appropriate solutions to address cash issues? Line of credit, capital leases, other long-term debt, equity financing, improved collections, slow payments or improving profitability.

info@ceocoaching.com   ceocoachinginternational.com

MONTHLY FINANCIAL REVIEW CHECKLIST
FOR HEADS OF FINANCE

QUESTIONS TO ASK WHEN BUILDING STATEMENTS AND CALCULATING METRICS

1. Who are the users of your Financial Reports? You should always consider the end users and their interpretation and needs when reviewing reports, ex. Board Members, Lending Institutions or Vendors. Any potential buyers for your business in the future should be kept front of mind as well.
2. Budgets are simply a picture at one point in time, although they are a key component of success and planning, you should be in continual evolution, evaluating changes in your business in real time so that you can adjust and adapt to change quickly. Using projection tools to compare to actuals and budgets to successfully position your team.
3. Are your financials completed and ready for review? Often owners/managers might view prior to completed close and create unnecessary concerns. Confirm the team has done their due diligence.
4. Are your accounts properly categorized? These can influence financial metrics required by lenders.
5. Point out unusual swings or targets below thresholds that should be reviewed and addressed.

KEY METRICS TO MEASURE

Profitability
☐ Revenue Growth
☐ Gross Profit (by product line, customer, job, etc.)
☐ Gross Profit % (whole company)
☐ Contribution Margin
☐ Operating Profit Margin %
☐ EBITDA Margin
☐ Breakeven Point
☐ Monthly revenue run rate
☐ Monthly nut (expenditures) that need to be covered
☐ Expense to Revenue Ratio
☐ Return on Equity
☐ Return on Assets

Efficiency
☐ Days Sales Outstanding
☐ Days Payable Outstanding
☐ Inventory Turnover
☐ Working Capital Turnover

Liquidity
☐ Current Cash Balance
☐ Cash Ratio
☐ Quick Ratio
☐ Current Ratio
☐ Number of months cash on hand
☐ Number of months inventory on hand

Solvency Ratios
☐ Debt Ratio
☐ Debt to Capital Ratio
☐ Interest Coverage Ratio

Solvency Ratios
☐ Debt Coverage Ratio
☐ Interest Coverage
☐ Fixed Charge Coverage

OTHER ANALYSES

1. Trend Analysis on all sections of your Profit and Loss should be conducted, assuring you know the drivers.
2. A product line and contribution margin analysis can be very beneficial to companies and can help them significantly improve their overall profitability. A revenue bridge is also helpful to understand why revenues are changing. What is due to changes in volume vs. changes in price?
3. Forecasting future cashflows to ensure you are meeting your working capital needs for the business especially if you have operational investments, growth expected or large capital expenditures.

info@ceocoaching.com   ceocoachinginternational.com

GOAL SCOREBOARD

Purpose

The Goal Scoreboard tool helps the owners of an initiative keep score on progress toward the goal. For sales purposes, it is also an integral part of the Sales Roadmap, Plan, and Playbook (SRPP).

> The more often you update your Goal Scoreboard, the more effective it is in making a difference on the business.

Instructions

Develop a highly specified scoreboard for the initiative at hand. Track the daily/ weekly/monthly trends in the leading indicator against the respective changes in the outcome. Compare the targets to actuals.

Tips

The more often you update your Goal Scoreboard, the more effective it is in making a difference on the business.

THE GOAL SCOREBOARD

ABOUT

How can you know if you're winning?

If you're only measuring outcomes instead of leading activities, then you have no way to hold yourself accountable in real time. The Goal Scoreboard tracks the drivers that move the needle in a key initiative, so you can see how your daily efforts impact the score.

THE TEMPLATE

	METRIC	TARGET	ACTUAL
OUTCOMES			
LEADING INDICATOR			
LEADING ACTIVITIES			

COMPLETED SAMPLE

	METRIC	TARGET	ACTUAL
OUTCOMES	PO $ RECEIVED	$150,000,000	$500,000
OUTCOMES	PO # RECEIVED	6	1
LEADING INDICATOR	QUOTES IN PIPELINE	15	8
LEADING INDICATOR	MEETINGS SCHEDULED	20	15
LEADING ACTIVITIES	CONVERSATIONS W/ QUALIFIED PROSPECTS	35	20
LEADING ACTIVITIES	PRESENTATIONS GIVEN	20	10

INITIATIVE COMMITMENTS TRACKER

Purpose

The Initiative Commitments Tracker helps teams focus on moving the needle on key initiatives by holding them accountable to specific and measurable weekly commitments.

Instructions

Update the weekly Initiative Commitments Tracker in advance of the weekly Move-the-Needle session. During the Move-the-Needle session, use the tracker as a guide for each member to

- share whether the commitments made last week were completed;

- review the impact of their actions on the leading and lagging indicators;

- unpack the root cause of any roadblocks and how they will overcome them in the future; and

- make a new commitment for the coming week.

Tips

A small number (one to two) of important commitments done well is better than many commitments that cannot all be kept or are done poorly. People are more likely to take real ownership of commitments they think of themselves. Keep day-to-day issues that are not related to the initiative commitments out of the meeting.

WEEKLY INITIATIVE
COMMITMENTS TRACKER
FOR MOVE-THE-NEEDLE SESSIONS

[Insert Initiative Name]

Goals		WEEK [#] Results
Specific & Measurable Outcome:	*From x to y by when*	
Hypothesis		
Leading Indicator #1	*From x to y by when*	
Leading Indicator #2	*From x to y by when*	
Leading Indicator #3	*From x to y by when*	

Team		WEEK [#] Commitment	Done?
Team Member 1	*Role*		
Team Member 2	*Role*		
Team Member 3	*Role*		
Team Member 4	*Role*		
Team Member 5	*Role*		
Team Member 6	*Role*		

CANDIDATE EVALUATION CHECKLIST

Purpose

The Candidate Evaluation Checklist helps you identify, select, and onboard world-class people who match your core values and have proven track records.

Instructions

Use the Candidate Evaluation Checklist during the interview process in conjunction with the Interview Scoring Matrix.

Tips

Hire an executive search firm to get access to the best pools of candidates.

CHECKLIST
CANDIDATE EVALUATION

You have to have the absolute best people on the team, so not surprisingly, this interview process is critically important to the future of your business. The right candidate will have a proven track record and share your company's values. If the candidate doesn't score high in both areas, say "next" and move on.

Interview Setup

☐ The entire Leadership Team should be involved in the hiring process of a C-Suite executive.

☐ Ask all candidates the same questions.

☐ Split up the range of topics among the members of the interview panel to ensure someone goes deep on all key areas.

Questions to Evaluate Track Record

☐ What Huge Outrageous Targets did you achieve in your past roles? (Dig deep here.)

☐ Imagine it is three years in the future and we are celebrating our accomplishments here. Describe what you see.

☐ Present a hypothetical 120-day strategic plan for our company. One of our current company issues is [insert]. What would you do?

Questions to Evaluate Values Alignment

☐ What type of culture do you think is the best fit for you?

☐ What does your ideal workplace look like?

☐ What business values are important to you?

☐ What do you find attractive about our company?

☐ What is your impression of our culture and what do you like/dislike about it?

☐ What do you think you could bring to our company that would mesh well with or complement our culture?

☐ Tell me about a prior work experience where you were not a strong cultural fit. Why was it a bad fit?

☐ What is success for you 5 years from now?

INTERVIEW SCORING MATRIX

Purpose

The Interview Scoring Matrix will help you make objective hiring decisions based on how well a candidate's prior work experience and values line up with the goals and values of your company.

Instructions

Ask the members of your interview panel to score each job candidate on a scale of one to five for each key criterion related to the position's required experience and each of your company's core values. Average the scores to see which candidate comes out on top.

Tips

If there is significant disagreement, have the interview panel discuss their differences to come to a consensus.

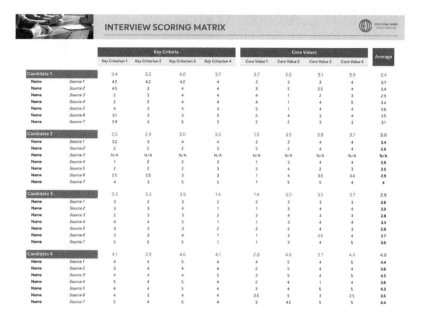

INTERVIEW SCORING MATRIX

		Key Criteria				Core Values				Average
		Key Criterion 1	Key Criterion 2	Key Criterion 3	Key Criterion 4	Core Value 1	Core Value 2	Core Value 3	Core Value 4	
Candidate 1		3.4	3.2	4.0	3.7	3.7	2.0	3.1	3.9	3.4
Name	Source 1	4.2	4.2	4.2	4	3	3	3	4	3.7
Name	Source 2	4.5	3	4	4	3	2	2.5	4	3.4
Name	Source 3	2	3	4	4	4	1	2	3	2.9
Name	Source 4	2	3	4	4	4	1	4	5	3.4
Name	Source 5	4	3	4	4	5	1	4	4	3.6
Name	Source 6	3.1	3	3	3	5	4	3	4	3.5
Name	Source 7	3.9	3	5	3	2	2	3	3	3.1
Candidate 2		2.5	2.4	3.0	3.5	1.5	3.5	3.8	3.7	3.0
Name	Source 1	3.2	3	4	4	2	3	4	4	3.4
Name	Source 2	2	2	2	3	2	2	4	4	2.6
Name	Source 3	N/A	N/A	N/A	N/A	N/A	N/A	N/A	N/A	N/A
Name	Source 4	1	2	2	3	1	3	4	4	2.5
Name	Source 5	2	2	2	3	2	4	2	3	2.5
Name	Source 6	2.5	2.5	3	3	1	4	3.5	3.4	2.9
Name	Source 7	4	3	5	5	1	5	5	4	4
Candidate 3		3.3	3.3	3.9	1.4	1.4	3.0	3.5	3.7	2.9
Name	Source 1	3	2	3	2	2	3	3	3	2.6
Name	Source 2	3	3	4	1	1	3	4	4	2.9
Name	Source 3	2	3	3	2	2	4	3	4	2.8
Name	Source 4	4	4	5	1	1	3	4	4	3.3
Name	Source 5	3	3	3	2	2	2	4	3	2.8
Name	Source 6	3	3	4	1	1	3	2.5	4	2.7
Name	Source 7	5	5	5	1	1	3	4	5	3.6
Candidate 4		4.1	3.9	4.6	4.1	2.8	4.6	3.7	4.4	4.0
Name	Source 1	4	4	5	4	4	5	4	5	4.4
Name	Source 2	3	4	4	4	2	5	4	4	3.8
Name	Source 3	4	4	4	5	3	5	4	5	4.3
Name	Source 4	5	4	5	4	2	4	1	4	3.6
Name	Source 5	4	4	5	4	3	4	5	5	4.3
Name	Source 6	4	3	4	4	2.5	5	3	2.5	3.5
Name	Source 7	5	4	5	4	3	4.5	5	5	4.4

LEADERSHIP TEAM 360° REVIEW

Purpose

The Leadership Team 360° Review allows leaders to receive candid, constructive feedback for developing their personal leadership and management skills.

Instructions

Ask team members to fill out the two-question template and submit their completed exercises to your coach, who will collect the anonymous responses and schedule a call to unpack the information with you. Use the feedback to determine your top three strengths and areas of improvement. Develop an applicable action plan with your coach and put an accountability system in place.

Tips

Giving feedback makes some people feel uncomfortable. Assure your team members that their responses will be anonymous, and follow through on that commitment.

LEADERSHIP TEAM
360° REVIEW

Please provide feedback for _____ by _____ / _____ / _____.

Return this form to _____ so that confidentiality is ensured.

Your responses are anonymous and will not be shared verbatim. Your feedback will be combined with many others, so the person being reviewed will not know who said what. Please contribute to the development of this person by being as direct and candid as possible!

Below are some categories that you may want to consider when providing your feedback, but please DO NOT BE LIMITED BY THESE SUGGESTIONS. Try to use specific examples of behaviors that you've observed whenever possible:

- Integrity in Communication
- The 3 C's of Communication (Clear, concise, compelling)
- Mentors and brings out the best in others
- Builds trust
- Teamwork & cooperation

- Work ethic
- Dedication & commitment
- Skill & knowledge
- Commitment to developing themselves
- Quality & accuracy
- Time management & effectiveness

- Attitude
- Dependability
- Takes initiative
- Adaptability & flexibility
- Judgement
- Leadership ability

1 Top 3-5 strengths (What do they do well?)

2 Top 3-5 opportunities (What could they do better?)

info@ceocoaching.com   ceocoachinginternational.com

POWER HOUR PLANNER

Purpose

The Power Hour Planner is a straightforward tool to help you gain better control of your own time, to your benefit and that of your team.

> If an important meeting gets scheduled at the same time, you can reschedule your power hour, but you cannot cancel it.

Instructions

Commit to carving time out of each day to focus on the most important activities that will drive the outcomes you want. Fill out the Power Hour Planner to make it official. Use this tool in conjunction with the Stop-Start-Continue tool to ensure that your Power Hour Planner is aligned with the best use of your time.

Tips

If an important meeting gets scheduled at the same time, you can reschedule your power hour, but you cannot cancel it.

POWER HOUR PLANNER

STEP 1 During your Power Hour, you'll focus exclusively on the three highest priority activities of the quarter. Write down those priorities below so you know exactly what to focus on.

1 |
2 |
3 |

STEP 2 Set a recurring calendar appointment each day of the week, whenever it is best for you. Every day doesn't need to have the same time slot. This is your Power Hour, your appointment with yourself. Like all appointments, Power Hour has a precise start and a precise end. In the scheduler below, decide when will be your Power Hour each day of the week.

	Sunday	Monday	Tuesday	Wednesday	Thursday	Friday	Saturday
5:00 - 6:00 am							
6:00 - 7:00 am							
7:00 - 8:00 am							
8:00 - 9:00 am							
9:00 - 10:00 am							
10:00 - 11:00 am							
11:00 - 12:00 pm							
12:00 - 1:00 pm							
1:00 - 2:00 pm							
2:00 - 3:00 pm							
3:00 - 4:00 pm							
4:00 - 5:00 pm							
5:00 - 6:00 pm							
6:00 - 7:00 pm							
7:00 - 8:00 pm							
8:00 - 9:00 pm							
9:00 - 10:00 pm							
10:00 - 11:00 pm							

STEP 3 Post your Power Hour Planner on the wall to hold yourself accountable to it. Inform your team when your Power Hour is, and request that they honor it. In Power Hour, no distractions are allowed: no phone, no email, no meetings, no interruptions.

CONTINUOUS LEARNING TRACKING SHEET

Purpose

Top performers understand that few things are more important to their success than being a lifelong learner. The Continuous Learning Tracking Sheet helps you organize the key areas where you need to focus your learning and map out a game plan to be a top student.

Instructions

Write down what you want to learn and where you can get that information. Define a deadline to gain that desired knowledge, in order to hold yourself accountable.

Tips

Define these priorities in conjunction with your coach. Distribute the tool throughout your whole organization to reinforce learning as a core part of your company's culture.

TRACKING SHEET
CONTINUOUS LEARNING

HOW TO USE IT

STEP 1 Identify your area of focus for continuous learning.

STEP 2 Identify the sources of info needed for each area of focus.

STEP 3 Identify the key insight that you desire.

STEP 4 Use the tool to hold yourself accountable. Decide a date to get it done by. Take searchable and easily accessible notes as you learn and frequently review the tracker to make sure you're learning the areas of focus you set out to learn.

TRACKING SHEET

AREA OF FOCUS	SOURCES OF INFO	DESIRED INSIGHT	DATE
Ex: Industry Developments; Technology; Management Best Practices; Competitors; Regulations	Ex: Industry conferences; Trade publications; Books; Someone in my personal network	Ex: "How to hire and inspire great people", "Forecasted impact of A.I. on the food service industry"	Date to hold yourself accountable to

info@ceocoaching.com   ceocoachinginternational.com

PART III

Integrating the MAKE BIG HAPPEN SYSTEM into Your Organization

In part II, we described the MAKE BIG HAPPEN SYSTEM in detail, showing you how you can leverage the system to MAKE BIG HAPPEN in your organization.

Here in part III, we discuss the common challenges our clients have faced integrating the MAKE BIG HAPPEN SYSTEM into their organizations:

- Hiring a Coach

- Getting Buy-In

- Starting Midcycle

- What If I Use Another "System"?

Hiring a Coach

Everyone needs a coach.
—*BILL GATES*

The MAKE BIG HAPPEN SYSTEM is logical and straightforward, but it is not easy, nor is it for the weary at heart. It requires persistence, assiduous devotion to the process, and a commitment to holding yourself and your team accountable to the activities that are identified by the system itself.

It should not be self-implemented. A humorous adage in the legal profession goes, "A lawyer who represents himself has a fool for a client." Ask yourself, "If I needed surgery, would I do it myself?" CEOs who go it alone deprive themselves of the guidance of someone who has achieved the same success to which they aspire, loses the value of an outside set of eyes to help them avoid the inevitable land mines, and have no one to hold themselves accountable to their own commitments. A CEO who serves as a facilitator at their strategic planning sessions is not acting as a faithful, objective, and full participant in the process.

Eleven-year CEO Coaching International client Andrés Jaramillo, CEO of Don Pedro's Kitchen, has had firsthand experience with the value of having a coach.

"In 2011, after having stabilized the business and being on the brink, my coach helped me craft our first strategic plan, which we named 'The 300-Forty Plan,'" Andrés shared. "We named it 'The 300-Forty Plan' because the goal was that by June 2011, we were aiming to reach $300,000 in revenue a month and a 40 percent gross margin."

In an effort to grow revenue and increase the value of his business, Andrés was focused on new product development, allocating significant time and capital to it. What Andrés did not see was that in his pursuit of product development, he was neglecting two crucial CEO responsibilities—key customer relationships and cash management. Because of it, the company suffered some months operating at a net loss.

Once Andrés's coach helped him see the roadblocks to his success, they pivoted and reprioritized. The small changes made a big impact.

"When we decided on 'The 300-Forty Plan,'" the goal was so big it seemed unimaginable. In August 2020, my coach and I celebrated a different milestone: in addition to the 40 percent gross margin, we exceeded $300,000 in net *profit*," Andrés said. "I am always asked and questioned by people close to me about the value of CEO coaching. Being able to say and knowing deep down that I am a much better entrepreneur today than I was before, and that my net profits have surpassed what my revenue goals were at the beginning of the coaching process, is the best proof I can think of as to the value of having a great coach."

Since implementing the MAKE BIG HAPPEN SYSTEM about a decade ago, Don Pedro's Kitchen has grown revenue and profit by more than ten times.

CEO Andrés Jaramillo (left) atop the Grand Canyon with CEO Coaching International founder Mark Moses (center) and Andrés's coach Michael Maas (right)

HOW TO CHOOSE THE BEST BUSINESS COACH FOR YOU

As a CEO, you are in demand. So why should you consider taking several hours a month out of your schedule to talk to a business coach? In a word—results.

The right business coach can make the difference between 3 percent growth and 33 percent growth. Between average profit margins and industry-leading profit margins. Between working all the time to taking time off and enjoying life. But how do you find that business coach who can make a massive difference in your life and in the results of your company?

Here is an eight-point checklist on what to look for in an effective business coach:

1. **Someone who has been there and done it.** It is hard to understand the ups and downs of being a CEO or entrepreneur unless you have been one yourself. For that reason alone, it is important to find a business coach who has walked in your shoes. You want a coach who has been on the hook for hiring and firing people, for meeting payroll, and for taking the business from idea to execution to generating profits.

2. **A clear best-practices methodology that gets results.** Coaching is not about winging it. Your coach should have a proven methodology that provides structure and direction while allowing your firm to personalize it based on your unique situation. Best practices work for a reason, and your coach should be steeped in them.

3. **A system to hold you accountable for getting things done.** Talk is cheap. You are not hiring a coach to have friendly chats. You are hiring a coach to get results. Make sure the coach you work with has a system that tracks action items and holds you and your team accountable for completing them.

4. **A process to help you determine what you want and the skill to identify the specific and measurable activities needed to get it.** It is easy to say, "Our goal is to grow 20 percent." It is much harder to determine the one or two

specific and measurable activities that, done consistently, will almost guarantee that you grow at least 20 percent. A good coach will challenge you on your goals and drive you to uncover the key activities that will make those goals a reality.

5. **The ability to help you see and overcome roadblocks to success.** We both know things do not always go as planned. Yet, the best business coaches have strategies to overcome many of the potential pitfalls that derail lesser entrepreneurs and CEOs. Take blind spots. We all have them, but you may be ignoring yours. A good business coach can shine a light on your blind spots and turn those liabilities into assets.

6. **A two-way fit.** Coaching can get extremely personal. A coach will get to know intimate things about their client's life. Take the time on the front end to make sure you and your business coach develop a trusting relationship. You do not have to be best friends, but you had better respect each other.

7. **The skill to shape you into a better leader.** Leaders can be made, and a top business coach can help you develop your leadership skills. If you want to build a great organization, you must be a leader people want to follow.

8. **Someone who has the courage to shoot you straight and call you out when you are acting or spewing nonsense.** Like I said earlier, your business coach is not designed to be your chat buddy. Coaching is about growing, developing, and getting results. When you are veering off course, your coach must have the confidence to bust your chops when needed.

Clearly, finding the right business coach is not something to take lightly. And the right coach does not come cheap. Yet, here is the deal:

the investment you make in working with the right business coach is irrelevant.

When you consider making a business investment, you run the numbers and look for a certain ROI. It is no different when hiring a coach. Do your homework. Ask the right questions. Use this checklist. When you find the right business coach, the fee they charge will be a small fraction of the return you receive in the form of revenue, profit, and personal growth.

Getting Buy-In

The fellow that agrees with everything you say
is either a fool or he is getting ready to skin you.
—*KIN HUBBARD*

Change is often met with skepticism. This is a natural reaction. However, without change, do not expect your performance to improve. Be prepared to spend time with key stakeholders and get their buy-in.

YOUR MANAGEMENT TEAM

Explain to your team that to achieve success, you need alignment, and to achieve alignment, you need a system. The MAKE BIG HAPPEN SYSTEM is a proven set of principles that give your management team a common language, healthy set of business rhythms, iterative framework, and a robust toolbox. Adopting the methodology across your whole team will enable you to execute more consistently and with higher satisfaction.

Dirk Bakhuyzen took over management of his Michigan-based family business PROCARE Landscape Management in April 2009. When we started coaching Dirk on the MAKE BIG HAPPEN SYSTEM in 2019, his brother Kyle, who also had a major stake in the business, spoke up and asked, "Why are you spending so much on coaching? This has to stop."

So, Dirk had Kyle hop on a coaching call with him. Once Kyle got a taste of the MAKE BIG HAPPEN SYSTEM, he understood the value and immediately signed up for coaching himself.

A few months later, another member of the PROCARE management team approached Kyle and said, "Why are you spending so much on coaching? This has to stop."

So—you guessed it—he had him hop on the phone with the coach, and once he got a taste of the MAKE BIG HAPPEN SYSTEM, he understood the value, and the questioning came to a halt.

If you are struggling to gain the buy-in of the other partners in your business, have them get on the phone with a MAKE BIG HAPPEN–certified coach to see the value for themselves. Having your other stakeholders get their own personal taste of the MAKE BIG HAPPEN SYSTEM is the most efficient way to score their buy-in.

Bakhuyzen brothers Kyle (left) and Dirk III (right) utilize the MAKE BIG HAPPEN SYSTEM to sustain year-over-year growth at PROCARE Landscape Management, founded by their father, Dirk Jr. (center).

YOUR BOARD

Boards of directors want to know that you are spending your time doing things of value that will grow the business. Let them know that by using the MAKE BIG HAPPEN SYSTEM, you are following a best-practices methodology developed by seasoned CEOs who have consistently outperformed their peers and often led to successful exits. The MAKE BIG HAPPEN SYSTEM holds the management team accountable. It helps a CEO optimize the business by providing a proven playbook for growth.

YOUR INVESTORS

Often private equity firms or other investors that have interest in a company have a laser focus on value creation. We know, since over 30 percent of our clients are private equity backed, and they appreciate having us create alignment and accountability across the management team. They expect extensive visibility into the business through frequent communication of progress on objectives and financial reporting.

Our longtime client Culmen International is a government contractor focused on international security, homeland defense, and humanitarian missions. In January 2020, a partial interest in the company was sold to New York-based growth equity firm Hale Capital Partners for $15+ million. After the transaction, the leaders at Hale Capital Partners worked with Culmen CEO Dan Berkon to use the Objectives and Key Results (OKR) framework developed by John Doerr to manage the business.

As Dan implemented OKRs, he saw that they were very helpful for setting goals and measuring results but fell short in the area of accountability. Knowing that the company's investors were expecting BIG results, Dan brought the MAKE BIG HAPPEN SYSTEM into the business and his coach ensured that Dan and his team stayed on track toward their goals.

Thanks to the concrete accountability that the MAKE BIG HAPPEN SYSTEM provides, Culmen has evolved from a mid-eight-figure company with modest profitability to a firm approaching $100 million in revenue generating greater returns to reinvest in the company and expand their capabilities with which to better serve their clients.

Unsurprisingly, the partners at Hale Capital have been extremely pleased and have adopted this system in other portfolio companies.

CEO Dan Berkon achieves buy-in from investors by continuously creating shareholder value at Culmen International.

If you ever need to gain buy-in from your investors, make sure they are aware that the MAKE BIG HAPPEN SYSTEM equips a CEO and their leadership team with many tools that will help keep them informed while enabling the management team to maximize enterprise value through superior growth in revenue and profit.

Starting Midcycle

You don't have to be good to start ... you just have to start to be good!
—*JOE SABAH*

There is never a perfect time to initiate change. That was the reality for CEO Chuck Green and his COO, Scott Robidoux, at their company, Assured Information Securities (AIS), a cyber and information securities firm operating in the highly regulated government contracting space.

It was April. Chuck knew he needed to move the company forward to hit his annual goals, and he was aware the current business system they were using was not producing the results they wanted. He also knew he could not afford to wait until the start of a new year to start making changes.

CEO Coaching International's Don Schiavone joined the AIS team to review the state of affairs together. Don saw everyone in the company was thoroughly busy with many tasks but did not have total clarity on the outcomes they wanted to achieve. Don started coaching Chuck and a small group of leaders, getting RHYTHM 5 in place, and familiarizing the team with the MAKE BIG HAPPEN SYSTEM. "Switching away from our previous business system wasn't difficult for us at all," Scott shared. "Even though we had five senior executive leaders, no one had been owning 'real' goals. With the MAKE BIG HAPPEN SYSTEM, having Don identify what was the whirlwind versus the important things we should be focusing on was a significant step in the right direction for us."

After getting one MAKE BIG HAPPEN RHYTHM under their belts, the next priority was for the leadership team to get alignment on what success looked like for their company and what the most important goals were for the next quarter. Don, Chuck, and the AIS team met in July for a quarterly alignment session that also served as a mini annual planning session for the rest of the year.

"The meeting created alignment for the team and exposed inefficiencies," said Scott. "By leveraging the CEO Coaching International techniques, we were able to refocus our strategy and operating model to address our concerns. We made significant progress, including turning an entire business unit toward profitability." With his renewed focus, he was able to coordinate sweeping changes in the business model, market focus, and client execution—a Q4 win with a BIG impact on their bottom line. By the end of the year, Chuck, Scott, and the AIS leadership team had fully adopted the MAKE BIG HAPPEN SYSTEM and all seven healthy business rhythms. They held their first full annual planning session across two days in January.

"We realized we weren't focusing on the right things," Scott reflected. "The other planning methods we had before helped us get things done that we would have gotten done anyway—nothing that moved the needle. We didn't see a big impact until we focused on real numbers, real data, and 100 percent put our VP of operations on the initiatives full time instead of just tackling the issues that randomly came up."

CEO Chuck Green leading a discussion with the AIS leadership team

While the description of the MAKE BIG HAPPEN SYSTEM starts with a cascading set of business rhythms, from biennial all the way down to daily, the reality is that most clients—like Chuck and Scott—do not adopt the system neatly at the top of this cascading process. Like most companies we coach, your firm is most likely midcycle in between quarters and months away from the next annual planning cycle.

That is OK! How do you eat an elephant? One bite at a time.

Like AIS did, we recommend immediately conducting a mini annual planning session that covers now through the rest of the year by applying the best practices from RHYTHM 2 to develop an annual plan. Next, get into healthy quarterly, monthly, and weekly business rhythms using MAKE BIG HAPPEN RHYTHMS 3–7 from that point on. In parallel, you can work in any missing elements of your core identity from RHYTHM 1 over the coming months.

Whatever you do, do not rush to use every tool haphazardly. The tools are most powerful when applied within the context of the appropriate business rhythm. Recall that chapter 3 provides a handy tool mapping chart to remind you of which business rhythms the tools are most applicable to.

Better yet, hire a business coach who has made BIG happen in their career and is practiced in leveraging the MAKE BIG HAPPEN SYSTEM to hold you accountable.

No matter what, like Chuck and Scott did, just get started. The worst thing you can do is put this book on a shelf, decide to wait until when you think the timing will be better, and continue with the status quo. Just like with anything you

> **The worst thing you can do is put this book on a shelf, decide to wait until when you think the timing will be better, and continue with the status quo.**

do in life, you will get out of the MAKE BIG HAPPEN SYSTEM only as much as you put into it. "By jumping right into using the MAKE BIG HAPPEN SYSTEM, we have been able to focus our attention and our efforts, allowing us to develop repeatable processes we can use across many clients. This makes our business a lot more scalable," Scott commented. "We know that if we really want to achieve our corporate vision, we have to stick to this system moving forward."

What If I Use Another "System"?

The union of opposites, in so far as they are
really complementary, always results in the most perfect harmony;
and the seemingly incongruous is often the most natural.
—STEFAN ZWEIG

Many of our clients are using other frameworks to help grow their business, such as EOS, OKR, 4DX, Scaling Up,[10] and other similar models. While there may be differences in approach between these

---

10   EOS, OKR, 4DX, and Scaling Up are registered trademarks of the respective companies.

frameworks and the MAKE BIG HAPPEN SYSTEM, we have found in practice that they are quite complementary.

We are, in fact, big fans of systems like these—namely, the healthy practice of getting teams organized around a vision, goal, and common definitions and a method for holding middle management accountable in an objective manner. When we begin working with new clients who already use these systems, we take tremendous satisfaction in knowing that their companies have typically done the heavy lifting of cleaning up some of their past bad practices, introducing objective measurements, and instituting a culture of goal attainment.

These business frameworks establish a shared vocabulary that fits easily into one or more of the MAKE BIG HAPPEN RHYTHMS. For example, the Objectives and Key Results (OKR) framework, made popular in *Measure What Matters*, by John Doerr, provides an excellent alternative for framing your annual and quarterly goals.

Contemporary Energy Solutions founder Tony Vlastelica is one client of ours who has been very successful with using OKRs layered with the MAKE BIG HAPPEN SYSTEM. Tony and his team adhere strictly to the OKR goal-setting structure while bringing in their MAKE BIG HAPPEN–certified coach to facilitate their annual planning sessions, quarterly alignment sessions, and bimonthly accountability meetings to help them focus on what is truly important and think BIG all the time.

CEO Tony Vlastelica

Our coaches have used just about every other business system and methodology throughout their careers. These systems often offer an initial burst of momentum, as the team gets organized around a common set of practices and a shared vocabulary. Ultimately, however, we have found that these other systems have diminished returns, due to suffering from one or more of the following vulnerabilities:

- **Mission creep.** CEO Coaching International partner Chris Larkins recalls stepping into the quarterly alignment session of a new client who had previously been relying on EOS alone. The company had almost thirty annual and quarterly "Rocks," as goals are called in EOS. "OK," Chris remarked, "which five or six of these do you actually want to achieve?" The idea that any organization could simultaneously focus on myriad goals is, as we all know, a fallacy. Yet, perhaps due to the inexperience of the facilitator or because of "self-facilitating," many companies fall into the trap of listing *everything* they could or want to do—and have a knack for making them all sound really important. For example, the marketing team might define the quarterly goal as "refresh the website." Who does not want a fresh website? But is it tied to the company's primary goal that year or even that quarter? Has the actual impact of that website refresh been objectively calculated? What should the marketing team's key area of focus be, if all their critical activities were laser focused on the HOT? "Mission creep," as we call it, might come from an unseasoned facilitator as suggested above or even from the nature of the process itself. If the pre-work of a quarterly meeting is "Each department must bring and report on its goals" instead of a rigorous structure to identify what is most important and what everyone should do about it, why should we be surprised?

- **Everything is a goal.** This is a similar problem to the above. If your CFO's quarterly outcomes or targets sound like "timely, accurate financials," you may wish to remind them that this is their day job, not a goal. The hypothetical CFO above should instead have a quarterly initiative that sounds much more like "Refresh the Cash Bridge Tool. Identify and deploy one or more initiatives to generate six months of cash on hand." The initiative of your head of sales might be "Conduct weekly role-play and training sessions with underperforming reps until the attachment rate of Product X increases to 25 percent, as identified in the Sensitivity Analysis." Your initiative as the CEO might be "Hold qualifying conversations with at least three smaller competitors in the southeast United States to gauge their interest as acquisition targets."

- **Not thinking big enough.** Is your team really pushing itself to achieve something difficult, something that would truly make you celebrate? Is it trying to influence events or just manage them? Does your process ask the right questions? Does it accept *standard* rates of growth? Do your sessions feel more like discussions of why big things *cannot* happen rather than active planning meetings to determine how we would achieve BIG results "if our lives depended on it," hypothetically, of course?

- **Not C-suite focused.** You adopted a new system to help your middle management get organized, collaborate with one another more frequently, and feel like they have a stake in success. These are outstanding reasons to adopt a system. Ask yourself, "Is it enough? Does it drive growth? Is it time to go further? Does my system allow me and my C-suite to think about *next* year while middle management focuses on this year?"

- **The honeymoon is over.** Many of our clients who implement these systems continue to use the vocabulary into tangible action through healthy cadences that helped them clean up their business rhythms. Observe, institute a culture of measurement, and make significant early gains. Most, however, observe that the honeymoon period tends to last between three months and a year, while the low-hanging fruit is picked.

Do you feel like you are now just going through the motions, like a bureaucratic agency following an SOP? Have greater growth and new powerful breakthroughs begun to elude you? We have seen and fixed the above weaknesses hundreds of times under the rubric of the MAKE BIG HAPPEN SYSTEM.

Many clients, in fact, come to us after having implemented another business "system" only to watch it go stale. They had struggled to figure out what to add to that system to drive extraordinary growth. The shared vocabulary of a "Rock" or an "Objective and Key Result" can transform a company only insofar as the company can choose the correct strategic focus and core activities to drive growth. Unfortunately, we frequently find companies that use these systems to organize no more than their daily activities, leaving the leadership team with the false satisfaction that they have cascaded a set of activities across the entire organization. Extraordinary growth only comes from a process that drives strategic thinking, combined with a relentless focus on the correct leading activities that move the growth needle.

The MAKE BIG HAPPEN SYSTEM forces the leadership team to focus on the activities that truly make an impact and change the trajectory of revenue and profit as opposed to organizing the day job of your teams. The MAKE BIG HAPPEN SYSTEM provides a flexible framework to GROW YOUR BUSINESS. Yes, a by-product is a shared vocabulary, a set of tools, and a set of common practices. However, the key difference is in our system's relentless focus on revenue and profit growth. Some systems will get you organized; the MAKE BIG HAPPEN SYSTEM makes you money.

Our client Trey Marler, CEO of Advance Body Scan, used EOS's framework before deciding to implement the MAKE BIG HAPPEN SYSTEM. So, being familiar with EOS's language, the Advance Body Scan leadership team continued to use some of their material, including referring to their "initiatives" as "Rocks." However, after learning about the MAKE BIG HAPPEN RHYTHMS, Trey and his team switched over to using our questions, structures, and tools, seeing that they led to better results in the business. There is no problem with this utilization of both systems. "It works seamlessly for us," Trey shared. "We have clarity in the organization and are growing like never before."

It is the flexibility of the MAKE BIG HAPPEN SYSTEM that separates it from the rest of the pack. This flexibility also requires a nuanced approach to adapt it to the unique needs of your business. Our tools are multipurpose and easily customizable to diverse challenges as they arise. We have seen the greatest impact when it is led by a certified MAKE BIG HAPPEN business coach who has already made BIG happen in their past career. Clients who have used the MAKE BIG HAPPEN SYSTEM for over three years have an average revenue CAGR of 18.6 percent—nearly two times the national average reported by the NYU Stern School of Business—and average EBITDA CAGR of 30.4 percent—over three times the national average. On average, this means that their revenue is doubling every four years, and their profit is doubling every three years.

PART IV

Conclusion—a
False Choice

*The world is moving so fast these days
that the man who says it can't be done
is generally interrupted by someone doing it.*
—*ELBERT HUBBARD*

Systems and philosophies are extremely powerful.

There are numerous systems to help you get organized. Without a powerful strategic call to action and a strong guiding hand, however, they can miss the mark, collapse under their own weight, and fall well short of growing your business to its maximum potential.

Many business philosophies are likewise profound and can generate huge growth. We are huge fans of the work of Jim Collins across a lifetime of publications. Similarly, we preach the wisdom of Renée Mauborgne and W. Chan Kim's *Blue Ocean Strategy*; Matt Dixon's *The Challenger Sale*; Patty McCord's *Powerful*; Chris McChesney, Jim Huling, and Sean Covey's *The Four Disciplines of Execution*; and other seminal books that have helped us all rethink how we conceive of and grow our businesses. We have cited many of these in this very book, and some of these authors have spoken at our annual CEO Coaching MAKE BIG HAPPEN Summit. However, without a holistic process to combine these insights into a single, disruptive strategy with momentum, accountability, and measurement, they often fail to do more than inspire a single great idea or initiative.

If a great system and insightful philosophies are powerful individually, together the combination of the two is exponentially greater. The MAKE BIG HAPPEN SYSTEM brings together the strengths of expert process and philosophies: it gets you organized *and* helps you grow, with our world-class CEO coaches and battle-tested tools. Opting for either a better rhythm, on the one hand, or bigger growth, on the other, is a false choice.

The annual, quarterly, monthly, and weekly rhythms pull from the best of multiple sources. They emphasize specific and measurable goals that are broken into manageable near-term milestones that feed long-term Huge Outrageous Targets (HOTs) and that are driven by initiatives with clear owners and definitions of success, fueled by expertly defined leading activities, and measured in real time. As coaches of your business, we deploy the MAKE BIG HAPPEN SYSTEM to utilize the right tools at the right time for the right reason to get results. With our proven methods that drive accountability and controlled change, we will not let distraction or lack of inspiration be your biggest enemies.

Sales strategies guided by the MAKE BIG HAPPEN SYSTEM drive significant growth. Led by a seasoned successful former CEO, the Revenue Bridge, Acquisition Growth Map, and Sensitivity Analysis reveal the biggest opportunities and pathways to success. The Sales Roadmap, Plan, and Playbook refines this further, converting vision and opportunity into specific stated assumptions, focus, and predefined key sales and marketing activities that can be measured and adjusted in real time, along with an effective script to guide performance.

Let us circle back to Bryce Maddock and Jaspar Weir's extraordinary journey in the foreword, from dreaming big while living in their parents' basements, to their company's extraordinary initial public offering (IPO) on Nasdaq less than ten years later, at an enterprise value in the BILLIONS.

Bryce and Jaspar launched an impressive business for a couple of twentysomethings, with TaskUs quickly exceeding $6 million in revenue and attracting initial offers to sell the business. They aimed for something considerably BIGGER—a $1 billion company. In 2014 they adopted the MAKE BIG HAPPEN SYSTEM, and through their focus and determination, TaskUs began to skyrocket.

In the first two quarters of 2015 alone, TaskUs doubled in revenue and headcount, capturing world-class clients like Uber, Tinder, Groupon, and HotelTonight. On the heels of this growth, they attracted the attention of a Philippines-based private equity fund, Navegar, whose partners were the founders of the call center outsourcing industry. Bryce and Jaspar secured a $15 million investment to fund their next phase of growth.

The Navegar investment was a huge win to celebrate, but the friends decided to think even BIGGER. Jaspar and Bryce doubled down, and TaskUs continued to grow at breakneck speed.

By 2018, TaskUs was contacted by the Blackstone Group—the largest PE firm in the world. Blackstone knew that ride sharing, social media, online food delivery, and other e-commerce businesses would continue to thrive, and would therefore ever increasingly depend on TaskUs for business support. Blackstone invested in Bryce and Jaspar's vision, and valued TaskUs at over $500 million. They were halfway to their billion.

In 2021, less than seven years after their billion-dollar quest began, Jaspar and Bryce's persistence and discipline paid off BIG. On June 11, 2021, the two founders stood at the Nasdaq closing bell in New York City to celebrate their hugely successful IPO. Initially expected to be valued at $23.00 per share, totaling $2.3 billion (230 percent greater than their target), they opened at $27.55 and soared 35 percent on opening day. Three days later, the company was trading at a valuation of $3.5 billion!

Bryce and Jaspar's outcome was certainly extraordinary in size, but in terms of their ability to set and achieve a gigantic goal, they are not alone. As observers and participants in all the success stories outlined in this book, we know firsthand that the MAKE BIG HAPPEN SYSTEM works. We know that the leaders cited herein all possessed an unswerving commitment to a methodology that accentuates several key traits:

- The harnessing of disruptive thought and provocative strategy

- A culture of deliberate planning and continuous measurement

- Access to world-class tools for forecasting and planning

- Commitment to healthy business rhythms structured to

emphasize learning and generate what Jim Collins would call a "flywheel effect" of ever-growing momentum

- An ongoing frequent process of examination, interpretation, and accountability

These leaders each began by identifying a long-term, life-changing outcome, the HOT—for example, "We will double the size of our business in three years, from $X to $Y." They further defined the specific and measurable results that would make them celebrate twelve months from now, as they will have achieved the first milestone of their tremendous journey. These leaders defined and communicated the specific and measurable results that would make them celebrate as they achieved the first and further future milestones of their journey. Based on that, they outlined where they needed to be in three months, to give them confidence that they would reach their next annual milestone—and critically, they did this every three months through rigorous strategic planning and quarterly reviews. They built systems to track and measure the impact of these actions, and to hold themselves accountable to their commitments and desired outcomes. Ultimately, by adhering to these practices, they identified the correct actions at each stage of growth. They avoided the biggest pitfalls, pivoted from mistaken good-faith assumptions and unforesee-able setbacks, eluded "shiny objects," and ultimately, they generated tremendous year-over-year growth.

Most companies never make it to eight or nine figures because they do not have a clear picture of where they want to go *and* a repeat-able system with specific and measurable activities that will get them there. The best companies follow a structured planning and execution framework that creates directional clarity and operational results. This is what we have captured in the MAKE BIG HAPPEN SYSTEM and have layered a set of expert-crafted tools on top.

Each step in the MAKE BIG HAPPEN SYSTEM requires observation, analysis, responsibility, and an openness to learning and adjusting if necessary. At each stage, significant customization takes place—applying provocative thinking to *your* business and *your* unique opportunities and challenges; assessing real-time resources, people, and conditions that affect your ability to achieve the desired outcome; and leveraging the strength of your team and your culture to bring your HOT into view.

The MAKE BIG HAPPEN SYSTEM was born from our own collective experiences running and turning around complex, successful businesses and enriched by the crowdsourced practice of having applied it to hundreds of companies around the world for the past thirteen years. It is designed to work for all businesses because it is built with a general, universally applicable framework. A seasoned and qualified practitioner can apply the right strategic and analytical tools on top of this framework to create a customized growth plan for any business. It works because it brings together *all* the conditions that success requires—strategy, meticulous planning, powerful tools, leading activities, a system to keep score, and an empowered team of the world's best talent—operating within a culture of accountability that drives constant innovation, achievement, and momentum.

So, read this book, but more importantly, "do the book." To quote the famous philosopher Yoda, "Try not. *Do*, or *do not*. There is no try." The MAKE BIG HAPPEN SYSTEM works for hundreds of businesses around the world, and it will work for you too. So, go forth and MAKE BIG HAPPEN.

ACKNOWLEDGMENTS

It is easy to acknowledge, but almost impossible to realize for long,
that we are mirrors whose brightness, if we are bright,
is wholly derived from the sun that shines upon us.
—*C. S. LEWIS*

This book is the culmination of over a decade of real-world testing in the field by more than eight hundred of our clients at CEO Coaching International. You helped us shape the MAKE BIG HAPPEN SYSTEM and refined the tools that have become the foundation for this book. Our sincere thanks must start with every one of you. We would like to specifically acknowledge the following:

- Bryce Maddock (CEO and cofounder) and Jaspar Weir (president and cofounder) of TaskUs

- Jim Bennett (CEO and founder) of Worldwide Express

- David Weingard (founder and executive chairman) of Cecelia Health

- Kerry Siggins (president and CEO) of StoneAge

- Siamak Taghaddos (CEO and cofounder) and David Hauser (CTO and cofounder) of Grasshopper

- Rob Posner (CEO) of NewDay USA

- Yi Li (CEO) of RNG International

- Josh McCarter (CEO) of Mindbody

- Kevin Duffy (CEO) of Sound United

- Rich Balot (CEO and founder) of Victra

- Heather Nichols (president) of Fluid Life

- Jamil Nizam (CEO) of Master Electronics

- Jan Bednar (CEO and founder) of ShipMonk

- Victor Santos (CEO and founder) of Airfox

- Rick Sapio (CEO) of Mutual Capital Alliance

- Tera Peterson (cofounder and CEO) of NuFACE

- Sarah Dusek (CEO) of Under Canvas

- Brad Caton (CEO and founder) of Invictus Professional Snowfighters

- Ron Carson (founder and CEO) of Carson Group

- Carol Clinton (CEO) of Timeless Skin Solutions

- Patrick Richard (founder and CEO) of Stoneweg US

- Rick Weber (CEO) of CBC Federal Credit Union

- Andrés Jaramillo (CEO) of Don Pedro's Kitchen

- Dirk Bakhuyzen (CEO) of PROCARE

- Dan Berkon (founder and CEO) of Culmen

- Charles Green (founder and CEO) and Scott Robidoux (COO) of Assured Information Securities

- Tony Vlastelica (founder) of Contemporary Energy Solutions

- Trey Marler (CEO) of Advance Body Scan

Of course, we would be nowhere without the tireless and generous work of our talented coaches, who are dedicated to MAKING BIG HAPPEN with their clients. We are continually amazed at the magic that happens when you put over thirty of the most accomplished former CEOs in a room and watch them passionately work with one another to help solve the challenges facing their clients. It is through these weekly group sessions within our firm whereupon the MAKE BIG HAPPEN SYSTEM, along with our suite of tools, was born. We would especially like to thank the following:

- Jason "Jay" Reid, for being the first coach to join the coaching team with Mark Moses. We affectionally refer to Jay as "patient zero."

- Sheldon Harris, for your passion for helping others be the best versions of themselves. You are a consummate coach and leader and have forever left your mark on CEO Coaching International.

- Jacquie Hart, for your commitment to building a world-class strategic partner community and helping clients, partners, and coaches make timely connections to MAKE BIG HAPPEN together.

- Rafe Wilkinson, Jerry Swain, David Sobel, and Gerry Perkel, for your leadership in helping our coaches grow. Everyone needs a coach! Rafe, Jerry, David, and Gerry apply patience and accountability to coach our coaching teams and enable them to thrive.

- Alberto Carvalho, for your strategic guidance and constant pushing to challenge us to MAKE BIG HAPPEN ourselves as a firm.

We must also thank our tireless support staff who work behind the scenes to keep the firm running smoothly. They have all contributed in their own way to the writing of this book. We would like to recognize the following team members who went above and beyond the call:

- Rachel Smith, for her ability to synthesize complex and often contradictory information to pull together our best practices and standard operating procedures that have become the foundation of the MAKE BIG HAPPEN SYSTEM. Rachel was also instrumental in developing the manuscript of this book and invested countless hours editing and reediting tools, client stories, and draft after draft of the book.

- Aubry Bracco, for her contributions to the many client stories that are woven throughout the book. Her ability to turn a client interview into a story worth reading is utterly amazing.

- Dawn Pope, for her many decades of dedication and support to Mark Moses through his many ventures and to her selfless support of the entire CEO Coaching International team.

- Steve Sanduski, for his leadership of our podcast series and capturing real-world stories of our clients MAKING BIG HAPPEN out in the field.

- Lorenzo Bizzi, PhD, for his brilliant consulting through the very early stages of this book as our business strategy professor and scholar in residence.

Finally, and most importantly, we would like to thank our families, who supported us throughout the years while we traveled the world helping our clients MAKE BIG HAPPEN and who most recently had to put up with our many late nights as we worked to get draft after draft of the book perfect. Without your support, none of this would be possible.

ABOUT THE AUTHORS

We are the products of editing,
rather than of authorship.
—*GEORGE WALD*

Mark Moses

Mark Moses is author of the international best-selling book *MAKE BIG HAPPEN* and the founding partner of CEO Coaching International, which coaches hundreds of the world's top high-growth entrepreneurs and CEOs in over forty countries. He has coached many CEO Coaching clients to nine- and ten-figure exits or valuations.

CEO Coaching International coaches CEOs on how to dramatically grow their revenues and profits, implement the most effective strategies, become better leaders, grow their people, build accountability systems, and elevate their own performance. Mark has won Ernst & Young's Entrepreneur of the Year award and the Blue-Chip Enterprise award for overcoming adversity. His last company ranked as the #1 Fastest-Growing Company in Los Angeles, and was number ten on the Inc. 500 list of fastest-growing private companies in the United States. CEO Coaching International has appeared on the Inc. 5000 list for the last seven consecutive years.

Mark has completed twelve full-distance Ironman Triathlons, including the Hawaii Ironman World Championship five times. He has also run marathons all over the world, including Antarctica and the Polar Circle Marathon. He also won the US National Squash Championship in 1992. Mark competed in the London Marathon in April 2019, qualifying him for the Boston Marathon. In May 2019 at the CEO Coaching International Summit, Mark had the honor of sitting down for an hour on stage with President George W. Bush to discuss entrepreneurship and life as president.

Mark served on the board of the Children's Hospital of Orange County for several years. He grew up in Canada and currently lives in Miami Beach with his wife, Ivette, and two children, Darien and Mason.

Mark is also a longtime active member of Young Presidents' Organization (YPO) and Entrepreneurs' Organization (EO) and has served as president of both organizations.

Don Schiavone

Dominic "Don" Schiavone spent over thirty years leading high-growth businesses using an in-depth understanding of technology and a data-driven "test-everything" philosophy. Don's motto is "You can't manage what you can't measure." His approach to coaching focuses on three pillars of success: people, process, and systems, in that order.

Throughout Don's coaching career, he has helped over twenty companies achieve extraordinary growth, with many clients leading to meaningful exits. Don currently leads CEO Coaching International as chief operating officer (COO) and managing director (MD), where he has been a driving force behind the formalization of the MAKING BIG HAPPEN system over the years.

Prior to coaching, Don led the growth of Grasshopper, the entrepreneurs' phone system, to a $172.5 million exit to Citrix, where he was coached by Mark Moses. Don was able to put the earliest version of the MAKE BIG HAPPEN SYSTEM into practice himself as a client and knows what it is like to be on the other side of the coaching relationship.

Don was awarded the Best New Mentor of the Year award from Boston TechStars and served as vice chairman of the Assabet Valley Chamber of Commerce. He earned an MBA from the Wharton School of the University of Pennsylvania. He also holds a BS in electrical and computer engineering from Clarkson University and an MS equivalent in nuclear engineering from Naval Nuclear Power School.

Don has completed a Half Ironman Triathlon and is an avid downhill skier and golfer. Don grew up sixty miles north of New York City, in a small town outside of Poughkeepsie, New York, and currently lives in the Boston suburbs with his wife, Natalie, and three children, Megan, Lauren, and Tyler.

Chris Larkins

Chris Larkins is a senior partner and chief growth officer at CEO Coaching International. In addition to serving as an active coach to over a dozen CEOs and their leadership teams, Chris leads a critical arm of the firm's growth by identifying and retaining new coaches—all of whom, as successful former presidents and CEOs themselves, have also made BIG happen.

Chris has always relished being told that something was impossible, only to find the way to prove skeptics wrong and accomplish it anyway. A natural challenger, he has a reputation for his willingness to question the conventional wisdom and thereby channel new insights into the development and execution of effective strategies for quick, significant impact. He has been recognized multiple times for taking organizations to number one in their spaces—including, as a turnaround hired gun, several "worst-to-first" transformations.

Chris is particularly known for creating world-class sales processes, playbooks, and teams that generate rapid revenue growth. He combines this with an unyielding commitment to operational excellence and customer experience. Chris believes that the costliest and most difficult thing for competitors to replicate is not a product or marketing campaign but rather flawless execution on everything from sales to operations.

His experience growing businesses across numerous industries and platforms makes Chris especially unique. Immediately prior to joining CEO Coaching International, Chris served dual roles as regional president and corporate COO of Prime Communications, AT&T's largest authorized retail chain, which tripled in size to six hundred locations during his tenure. He built the engine that produced record gross profit across the enterprise and the operational infrastructure to support the tripling of the company's footprint in less than three years.

Chris has over twenty years' experience serving as president or managing partner of numerous companies in consumer services, distribution, manufacturing, and international business. He has established supply chains and subsidiary operations around the globe, particularly in Latin America and India. In all cases, Chris proved himself to be a powerful renovator and an agent for change—leading aggressive turnarounds of distressed companies and/or helping them transform their businesses in the face of adverse market conditions or deteriorating performance.

Chris earned a PhD in public law from the University of Southern California, participated in World Bank projects in Argentina and Peru, and was published and widely cited in leading peer-reviewed journals. He is a longtime highly engaged member of YPO, where he is widely known for leadership roles globally, regionally, and locally. During his tenure as chairman, the YPO Orange County Chapter was rated number one worldwide, out of four hundred chapters across the globe. Originally from Philadelphia and a lifelong Phillies fan, Chris and his family enjoy international travel together, especially to Spain and Italy.

Craig Coleman

Over the last twenty-five years, Craig's career has taken him from corporate attorney to investment fund principal to entrepreneur to CEO coach. This journey has taught Craig to look at businesses from multiple perspectives and to observe different leadership styles and their effectiveness. Craig believes that success as an individual, or as an organization, comes from combining passion with focus and discipline.

At CEO Coaching International, Craig is a coach and member of the firm's executive team. Craig's clients include an array of businesses in a variety of industries, including SaaS, consumer and commercial lending, private equity, manufacturing, defense contracting, and live event promotion. Craig believes that leadership is a sacred responsibility because leadership, good or bad, has long-term, wide-ranging impact. He is a true believer in the value of coaching and the importance of continual self-improvement. Having formerly been a CEO Coaching International client for six years, Craig credits coaching with helping him become a more self-aware and effective leader.

Prior to coaching, Craig cofounded ForwardLine Financial, a nationwide small business lender, and ForwardLine Payment Services, a full-service payment processor. During Craig's tenure as CEO, ForwardLine raised over $100 million in capital and experienced fifteen consecutive years of growth, growing to $400 million in combined annual volume. In 2015, Craig led the successful sale of both companies to a private equity firm.

Prior to founding ForwardLine, Craig served as a principal at a boutique finance company specializing in bridge loans and minority equity positions in emerging companies. He began his career as a corporate attorney at O'Melveny & Myers and Skadden, Arps, Slate,

Meagher & Flom specializing in mergers and acquisitions and commercial debt transactions.

Craig holds a BA in economics with high honors from Boston College and a JD with honors from Georgetown University Law Center. He has been a frequent speaker at industry conferences as well as a guest lecturer at the USC Marshall School of Business, Loyola Marymount University, and West Los Angeles Community College. Craig lives in Pacific Palisades, California, with his wife, Molly, and their three sons, where they enjoy an active Southern California lifestyle. Craig regularly volunteers his time serving his community. He has served on the board of Corpus Christi Parish School and is an active member of Corpus Christi Parish. He is also an Eagle Scout and serves on the Western Los Angeles County Council for the Boy Scouts of America.

INDEX

The mind's cross indexing puts the best librarian to shame.
—SHARON BEGLEY

C

G

H

I

L

M

O

T

U

V

W